# How to Pass

D1644689

SECOND EDITION

## NATIONAL 5

# Art & Design

Elaine Boylan and
Stephanie Lightbown

HODDER GIBSON
AN HACHETTE UK COMPANY

The Publishers would like to thank the following for permission to reproduce copyright material:

**Photo credits p.21** (top left) © The Barnes Foundation, Merion, Pennsylvania, USA/The Bridgeman Art Library, (bottom left) © Lefevre Fine Art Ltd., London/The Bridgeman Art Library, (right) © Private Collection/The Bridgeman Art Library; **p.23** © Private Collection/The Bridgeman Art Library; **p.28** (top left) © Succession Picasso/DACS, London 2018 via AKG Images, (centre left) © Ken Currie/National Galleries Scotland/Presented by Stephen Baycroft and Donald Holt 2004, (bottom left) © Ken Currie, (top right) © Succession Picasso/DACS, London 2018 via AKG Images; **p.44** © German/iStockphoto; **p.56** (bottom left) © Kimberly Reinick – Fotolia.com; **p.57** (centre left) © Microsoft clipart, (bottom left) © Jaysen Baboolall, (centre right) © VeronikaMaskova/Shutterstock; **p.59** (top right) © MOURON CASSANDRE._www.cassandre-france.com, (bottom left) © Federal Art Project, ca. 1941. (Library of Congress, Prints & Photographs Division, WPA Poster Collection, LC-USZC4-5064), (bottom centre) © Federal Art Project, ca. 1938. (Library of Congress, Prints & Photographs Division, WPA Poster Collection, LC-USZC2-5301; **p.66** (top left) © Hedley, Gwen. *Drawn to Stitch* (2010). Reproduced with kind permission of B. T. Batsford, part of Pavilion Books Company Limited, (bottom centre) © Antonio de Moraes Barros Filho/WireImage via Getty Images; **p.67** (centre left) © Stefanie Nieuwenhuyse, (bottom left) © Sevenarts Ltd / DACS 2018 via Bonhams, London, UK/Bridgeman Images; **p.88** (centre left) © The Trustees of the British Museum, (centre right) © Kseniia/stock.adobe.com; **p.90** (top left) © The Henry Moore Foundation. All Rights Reserved, DACS / www.henry-moore.org 2018 via Tracey Whitefoot/Alamy, (centre left) © James Gardiner/SCRAN, (centre right) © 2000 Claes Oldenburg and Coosje van Bruggen; **p.91** (top left) © Glasgow Museums/SCRAN, (centre left) © Estate of Roy Lichtenstein/DACS 2018 via The Bridgeman Art Library, (centre right) © The Trustees of the British Museum; **p.93** (top left) © The Fleming-Wyfold Art Foundation/Courtesy of the Artist's Family/The Bridgeman Art Library, (top right) © Glasgow Museums: The Burrell Collection/Scran, (bottom left) © National Galleries of Scotland/SCRAN; **p.94** (centre left) © The Trustees of the British Museum, (top right) © Philadelphia Museum of Art, The Louise and Walter Arensberg Collection, 1950, Accession Number 1950-134-95; **p.95** (top left) © Mr S. Campbell/SCRAN, (top right) © Copyright the artist's estate/Scottish National Gallery of Modern Art/SCRAN; **p. 97** (top left) © Dorothea Langue/US Federal Government Archives, (centre right) © The Stapleton Collection/Bridgeman Art Library, (bottom left) © Martin Parr/Magnum Photos; **p.106** (top left) © James Gardiner/SCRAN, (bottom left) © Studio H/Doves Farm Foods Ltd, (bottom left) © Studio H/Doves Farm Foods Ltd, (bottom right) © Victoria and Albert Museum, London/V&A Images – All rights reserved; **p.108** (top left) © Victoria and Albert Museum, London/V&A Images – All rights reserved. (top right) © V&A Images – All rights reserved. (bottom right) © National Museums Scotland/SCRAN; **p.111** (top & centre left) © Royal Fine Art Commission for Scotland/SCRAN, (top right) © Joseph Sohm, Visions of America/Getty Images, (centre right) © Jeff Millies/Hedrich Blessing/ Arcaid/Getty Images; **p.113** (top left) © The Trustees of the British Museum, (centre left) © Victoria and Albert Museum, London/V&A Images – All rights reserved. (centre right) © National Museums Scotland/SCRAN; **p.115** (top left) © Liz Vandal, Cirque du Soleil, (bottom left) © Victoria and Albert Museum, London/V&A Images – All rights reserved. (bottom right) © storm – Fotolia.com; **p.126** (top left) © akg-images/Erich Lessing, (centre left) © De Agostini Picture Library/G. Nimatallah/The Bridgeman Art Library, (top right) © The Trustees of the British Museum, (bottom right) © By Michael Graves for Alessi.

**Acknowledgements pp.25, 32, 63, 70** Instructions to candidates taken from SQA portfolio evaluation forms. Copyright © Scottish Qualifications Authority.

Every effort has been made to trace all copyright holders, but if any have been inadvertently overlooked the Publishers will be pleased to make the necessary arrangements at the first opportunity.

Although every effort has been made to ensure that website addresses are correct at time of going to press, Hodder Gibson cannot be held responsible for the content of any website mentioned in this book. It is sometimes possible to find a relocated web page by typing in the address of the home page for a website in the URL window of your browser.

Hachette UK's policy is to use papers that are natural, renewable and recyclable products and made from wood grown in well-managed forests and other controlled sources. The logging and manufacturing processes are expected to conform to the environmental regulations of the country of origin.

Orders: please contact Bookpoint Ltd, 130 Park Drive, Milton Park, Abingdon, Oxon OX14 4SE. Telephone: (44) 01235 827720. Fax: (44) 01235 400454. Lines are open 9.00–5.00, Monday to Friday, with a 24-hour message answering service. Visit our website at www.hoddereducation.co.uk. If you have queries or questions that aren't about an order, you can contact us at hoddergibson@hodder.co.uk

© Elaine Boylan, Stephanie Lightbown 2018

First published in 2018 by

Hodder Gibson, an imprint of Hodder Education,

An Hachette UK Company,

211 St Vincent Street

Glasgow G2 5QY

| Impression number | 5 | 4 | 3 |
|---|---|---|---|
| Year | 2022 | 2021 | 2020 |

Cover photo © Hayati Kayhan/stock.adobe.com

Illustrations by Aptara, Inc.

Typeset in Cronos Pro by Aptara, Inc.

Printed in Spain

A catalogue record for this title is available from the British Library

ISBN: 9781510420823

# Contents

> The book you are holding is from a third (or subsequent) printing of this title. In this version, several changes (including marks) were made to the question paper section following minor SQA course amendment in late 2019.

# Introduction

This book is designed to help you to complete your art and design coursework successfully and to help you prepare for the written examination. It should help you to understand the course structure and how marks are allocated. A unique aspect of this book is the guidance which is included on the practical aspects of the course, which account for 80% of the marks.

## Advice to users

The book contains overviews of the key aspects of the National 5 Art and Design course:

Expressive activity with integrated critical studies

Design activity with integrated critical studies

Question paper

These sections will outline the process you should follow in order to fulfil the assessment standards. Expressive and design techniques are also included to help you when you are developing your own practical work.

### Case studies

In each section, case studies are shown to give you further insights into the course and to give ideas of different approaches. These have been developed from real students' work. The work used is of a particularly high standard so that you can see what good-quality work at this level might look like.

In art and design, there are no right or wrong answers – it is not like maths! It is important that you understand that there are many different ways of achieving the assessment standards. The case studies should help you to develop your own ways.

We have deliberately selected case studies in popular areas of expressive art and design. Although it is impossible to cover every type of portfolio within the scope of this book, whichever area you are working in, you will be able to gain inspiration and ideas which you can apply to your own work.

## External assessment – the portfolio gallery

A unique feature of this book is that it contains a visual representation of what portfolios look like when they are hung up for external marking. This should let you see how different formats work and to see how important it is that your own portfolio has visual impact and coherence.

## Feature boxes

### HINTS & TIPS

Examiner's tips are included throughout the book. This advice should help you to maximise your **marks.**

### COMMON MISTAKES

Throughout the book, alerts will be given on **problems** which cause candidates to lose marks.

### Teacher's feedback

Throughout the case studies, there are teacher's notes to let you see the feedback given at various stages. This should help you to understand the process followed by the candidate.

## National 4

Throughout the book, guidance is given for National 4 candidates, where there is a difference in requirements. Although there are some differences, National 4 students can follow much the same process as those doing the National 5 course. National 4 candidates who follow the guidelines given in this book for the expressive and design practical activities with integrated critical studies should overtake the assessment standards for National 4 (as long as the work is of the required quality).

The main differences for National 4 candidates are:

- There is no written exam
- Work is internally assessed so a portfolio does not have to be submitted
- Assessment is on a pass/fail basis
- Work will be levelled at SCQF level 4 rather than 5.

# Chapter 1

# Course Structure

| COMPONENT | ASSESSMENT ARRANGEMENTS | | MARKS AVAILABLE |
|---|---|---|---|
| Expressive activity | Portfolio | External assessment | 100 |
| Design activity | Portfolio | External assessment | 100 |
| Question paper | Examination | External assessment | 50 |
| | | TOTAL | 250 |

## Percentage of marks for each component

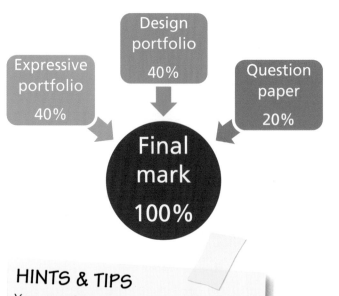

Expressive portfolio 40%

Design portfolio 40%

Question paper 20%

Final mark 100%

### HINTS & TIPS

Your portfolios are sent for external assessment. During the course, you might complete some work which is not included. This work will often consist of less successful pieces or ideas which you decide not to take forward.

### National 4

As there is no examination at National 4 level, your assessment is based on the practical and critical work you have carried out in your expressive, design and added value units. This work is assessed on a pass/fail basis. Although you only need to meet the minimum standard to pass, you should try to do your best possible work. This will be to your advantage if you progress to National 5 later, as your skills will be more developed.

# Skills and knowledge

In this course, you are being assessed on your ability to:

respond to a theme or brief in an effective and imaginative way

communicate personal thoughts, feelings and ideas

demonstrate problem-solving, critical-thinking and decision-making skills

plan, develop, produce and present creative art and design work

reflect on and evaluate art and design work

use art and design materials, techniques and technology in a creative and skilful way

understand how artists and designers use materials and techniques for creative and visual effect

understand the influence of social and cultural factors on art and design practice

# Time management

Good time management is key to achieving success in the course. It doesn't matter how talented you are, if you don't get the work done in time, your grade will be badly affected. Your teacher has to submit your work for assessment, and will instruct you to have your work completed well ahead of the SQA deadline. This is to allow your work to be checked and labelled. There are also important departmental quality assurance and administration procedures to be carried out.

## HINTS & TIPS

You are probably studying several subjects which will have coursework deadlines at the same time. You may be under a lot of pressure in March and April. You can avoid this stress by completing work for the interim deadlines given by your teacher.

Schools deliver the course in different ways, but your school will probably use one of the following three models:

Your school may cover the design activity first followed by the expressive activity:

Design portfolio and design studies → Expressive portfolio and expressive art studies

You might do the expressive activity followed by the design activity:

Expressive portfolio and expressive art studies → Design portfolio and design studies

Some schools do both activities concurrently. This means that you will complete your expressive and design activities at the same time, dividing your lessons each week between both:

Expressive portfolio and expressive art studies

Design portfolio and design studies

It doesn't matter which way your school delivers the course, but you should ensure that you are aware of key deadlines and which tasks are expected to be completed. Use the table on the following page to record your main deadlines. If you have not been given this information, ask your teacher.

You will also find that the expressive activity and design activity checklists in this book will help you to keep track of your progress and make sure you have completed all of the tasks required.

# Homework

Your teacher may give you specific homework tasks which will help you work towards completing your expressive and design portfolios on time. If you are struggling to complete tasks in class time, consider doing some extra homework. Ask your teacher what you are allowed to take home to complete.

If you are not given homework, there are many tasks which you can do at home to save time in class and help you to produce good-quality portfolios.

Homework tasks which you could do might include:

- market research for design
- research on related artists and designers
- initial sketch ideas for your design and expressive portfolios
- line drawings for your expressive portfolio which can be worked on in class.

Use your initiative! Refer to the case studies and advice on techniques in this book to develop your own work.

## HINTS & TIPS

When you are setting aside time for a task, work out how much time you think you need, then double it – practical tasks always take longer than you think!

## HINTS & TIPS

Make sure that you leave plenty of time for the final expressive outcome and design solution. It is important that you achieve the highest level of finish that you can. This should be the best work you have ever produced!

| KEY DEADLINES | | | |
|---|---|---|---|
| | Task | Date | ✓ |
| **Expressive activity** | | | |
| Portfolio | Selection of theme/stimulus | | |
| | Investigation and research | | |
| | Development | | |
| | Final piece | | |
| | Evaluation | | |
| | **Presentation of expressive portfolio** | | |
| **Design activity** | | | |
| Portfolio | Design brief | | |
| | Investigation | | |
| | Market research | | |
| | Development | | |
| | Design solution | | |
| | Evaluation | | |
| | **Presentation of design portfolio** | | |
| **Expressive art and design studies question paper** | | | |
| Question paper | Expressive art studies | | |
| | Design studies | | |
| | **Prelim exam** | | |
| | **SQA exam** | | |

Chapter 2

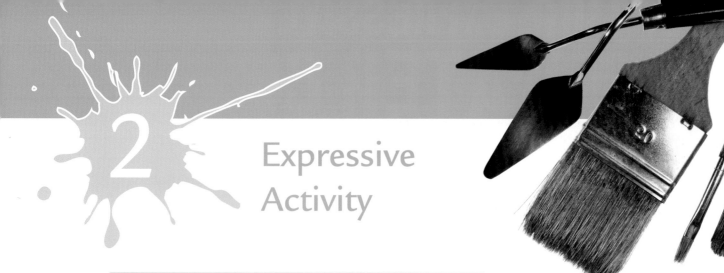

# 2 Expressive Activity

## Introduction and overview

### What is expressive art?

Expressive art is about communicating your own personal ideas in a visual way. There are a variety of expressive media, techniques and approaches to choose from and these should reflect the artist's personal preferences and style.

### What will I be doing in this activity?

#### The creative process

In your expressive activity, you will be following a **creative process:**

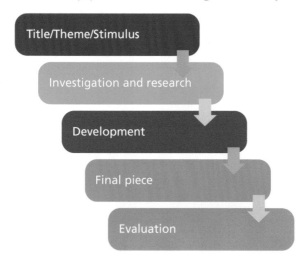

Title/Theme/Stimulus

Investigation and research

Development

Final piece

Evaluation

You will be producing a **portfolio** of expressive artwork in response to a **title**, **theme** or **stimulus**.

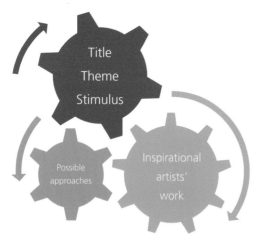

Title Theme Stimulus

Possible approaches

Inspirational artists' work

### National 4

You will follow a similar creative process and you can use the same starting points suggested for National 5.

Be careful to choose an achievable topic as you are still developing your basic expressive skills at this level.

## Responding to a theme or stimulus

Themes suggest a variety of things to different people and allow you to make a **personal** response.

It is a good idea to have a title as a starting point for your project, as this will help give it direction. Genres themselves are not titles. For instance, 'Still Life' or 'Portraiture' would not be suitable, as they are far too open-ended and don't suggest anything in particular.

You should choose a title, phrase or image which suggests visual ideas, such as 'Living in a Fantasy World', 'On Closer Inspection', 'Reflections', 'Deep in Thought', 'Breakfast', 'Urban Decay', 'Childhood Memories', 'Collection', 'Afternoon Tea', 'Making Music', 'Me, Myself and I'. The possibilities are endless!

Alternatively, you could use a **stimulus**. This could be an object or a place. Maybe a line from a poem or song could provide inspiration. Your starting point could perhaps be an artist's work or a photograph which you like.

## HINTS & TIPS

Your teacher may supply a choice of titles/themes/stimuli, or you may be asked to come up with your own idea. Make sure that you choose something you find genuinely interesting and which gives you lots of visual ideas.

## Working within a genre

You might choose to work within one particular **genre** (category):

**PORTRAITURE**

or

**FIGURE COMPOSITION**

or

**STILL LIFE**

or

**THE NATURAL ENVIRONMENT**

or

**THE BUILT ENVIRONMENT**

## Working across genres

You may also choose to work across genres, for instance producing:

- a portrait set in a built environment
- a still life set in the natural environment
- a figure composition in a landscape
- a fantasy scene incorporating aspects of several genres.

Another important aspect you will need to think about at the outset is the **approach** you will take. Your teacher will advise you about what is realistic. You may want to think about (or ask your teacher):

- Will this project be about 2D or 3D work or a mixture of both?
- Which **techniques** will I be using? (e.g. painting, drawing, print-making, mixed media, sculpture, low relief)
- Do I need to provide the **subject matter** (e.g. objects, images, photographs), or will departmental resources be available?

**NOTE:** Your teacher may offer you a limited choice. This is because departments often specialise in one or two areas which they have the expertise, equipment and resources to deliver. This ensures that you get the support and resources that you need to complete the project.

Your teacher also has to consider your level of skill and make sure that you don't attempt something that will be too far beyond your ability and experience.

## HINTS & TIPS

As well as researching and writing about artists, you could try to copy their style in a piece of work of your own. This is a great way to help you understand an artist's technique.

You will also complete some **expressive art studies** work. This should be related to the approach and subject matter you have selected. The expressive art studies tasks will help you to understand some key issues in expressive art and to develop your own approaches and techniques.

Your teacher will probably suggest some appropriate artists and artworks for you to investigate and analyse. Refer to the case studies to see how other candidates have approached this and to the section on the question paper.

# Successful artists are:

## Receptive to new experiences

Expressive art is like taking a journey without a map. You should be willing to explore, try new techniques, see what happens and where the journey takes you. Don't be too fixed in your thinking.

## Observant

To produce successful artwork, it is necessary to have good observational skills. This will help you to notice the qualities of the different subjects you are looking at, and to learn how to use techniques effectively.

## Focused

Expressive art requires a high level of concentration. Often, when you reach this level of focus, you will find that time seems to pass very quickly. Some people call this being 'in the zone'.

## Committed and engaged

You will feel frustrated at times. Sometimes things won't work out. This is all part of the process of discovery, so try to see the positive side. Perhaps a technique isn't for you, or you don't have enough experience with it yet. Keep trying and don't give in!

## Good at taking advice without taking it personally

If you feel as if you've put your heart and soul into something only to be told of its faults, it can be difficult. Remember, your teacher is giving you constructive advice. Try to bear in mind that any criticism is about your work, not you, so take it positively and move on.

## Self-critical

Push yourself to produce your best work. Students often think they are finished when there is more to be done. Try to notice missing details and whether tonal values are correct without having to ask your teacher.

## Creative

Some expressive approaches seem to allow for more creativity than others but, whatever your choice of subject, it is important to demonstrate that you can work in an imaginative way, particularly in the development stage of the process. This could be something as simple as trying different viewpoints in a still life composition, or varying your media.

## Willing to put the time in to improve and develop their own style

The only way to get better at drawing and a variety of expressive techniques is to practise. Unfortunately, there are no shortcuts! As well as noticing that your accuracy increases, you should find that your pace of work improves and that your confidence grows. The more you practise, the more likely it is that you will notice your own style developing.

## Investigation and research

**Subject matter**

What subject matter would be appropriate for my theme?

Can I identify appropriate primary/first-hand source material?

Do I need to take photographs or find secondary source material?

**Theme**

Which artists will inspire and influence my work?

What style will it be?

Which key visual elements interest me the most?

Consider:
- colour
- line
- tone
- shape
- form
- pattern
- texture

Will I work within one genre or work across genres?

What would be an appropriate scale for my work?

**Style and approach**

**Media and technique**

Which media might be appropriate? Consider:
- wet/dry media
- pencil
- paint (tempera paste, watercolour, acrylic)
- ink
- soft pastels
- oil pastels
- collage
- mixed media
- print-making
- sculpture, etc.

How will I present my investigation and research visually to show evidence of what I have done? Consider:
- personal observational drawings
- cuttings/photographs
- experiments with media/techniques
- examples of artists' work
- annotations

Where will I find what I need?

## Development and final piece

**Initial ideas**
- Consider a number of different possibilities in response to your theme

**Selection of best idea**
- Evaluate work done so far to see which idea is the best – remember to consider your theme
- Select the best idea for development

**Development and refinement of selected idea**
- Experiment with composition – think about viewpoint and arrangement
- Explore media techniques

**Final piece**
- Decide on the most successful approach in terms of composition, materials and techniques
- Decide on scale
- Carry out further refinement to your idea to improve composition, lighting, technique, media handling, for example

## Evaluating expressive work

Evaluation is an important aspect of your work. It is also a task many people find difficult. This section will help you to understand the purpose of evaluation and will help you to build your skills in this area.

Evaluation involves making judgements and giving reasons. It can be about:

■ what worked well
■ what went wrong
■ how successful or unsuccessful it is
■ advantages and disadvantages of an approach
■ whether everything went to plan, or why it didn't
■ how well you managed your time
■ the effectiveness of decisions you made
■ how well an outcome reflects the theme
■ whether you would approach a similar task in a different way in future
■ skills that you developed.

## What should I evaluate in my expressive portfolio?

The creative process – effectiveness of decisions made when working through your portfolio

The effectiveness of the visual qualities of your portfolio

### HINTS & TIPS

Try to vary your vocabulary so that your comments are not repetitive. You could use the wordbanks in Chapter 5 of this book or refer to a thesaurus. Developing your vocabulary will help you communicate your thoughts more clearly.

### COMMON MISTAKES

Instead of evaluating, students sometimes describe their work, or tell the story of what they did. This is *not* evaluation.

Your evaluation **must** be completed on the SQA evaluation template which can be downloaded from their website: www.sqa.org.uk/sqa/47388.html. There is no word count limitation as such, but you cannot exceed the space provided and the font size is locked. Therefore, it is recommended that your comments are very focused and concise.

When completed, your evaluation **must** be attached to the first sheet of your expressive portfolio.

## How to develop descriptive comments into evaluative comments

| BASIC AND DESCRIPTIVE COMMENT | EVALUATIVE COMMENT |
|---|---|
| My work is based on the title 'On Closer Inspection'.<br><br>Tell us a bit more. | I chose the title 'On Closer Inspection' as it gave me lots of creative possibilities. I decided to interpret the title by developing some close-up still life ideas as I enjoy drawing objects and I like detail. |
| I used photography during the development stage.<br><br>How did this help you? | I found using photography to develop compositions helped me to frame the objects and try different arrangements. This was a quick method which helped me decide which compositions I wanted to develop further. |
| My final piece is done using tempera paste.<br><br>The marker can see this. | I found tempera paste difficult to control at first, but as you can see in my final piece, I am now more confident and able to show tonal values and detail effectively with this medium. I also like the vibrant colour and brushwork. |
| I made a drawing of a red pepper.<br><br>We can see this! | For one study I decided to cut the red pepper in half as it gave some extra detail and made this line drawing more interesting. |
| I added a background to my portrait.<br><br>Why, and for what effect? | I was inspired by the artist Joan Eardley to try a collage background technique. I developed the idea of a graffiti wall as a background and used some of her techniques to achieve this. I feel this gives an urban feel to the work and fits with my theme of 'Street Life'. |
| I used a 3D mixed-media technique here.<br><br>Expand on this. | I used some found objects in this work to explore a 3D mixed-media technique as I was inspired by the work of Will Maclean in my expressive art studies. |
| I am happy with my expressive outcome.<br><br>You need to give reasons. | My final piece worked out well. I like the way I incorporated the figure into a rundown urban background as this adds a 'story' to the picture and reflects my theme of 'Down and Out'. The downcast expression of the subject also helps convey a despondent mood. |

# How your expressive activity relates to your portfolio

**Expressive coursework**

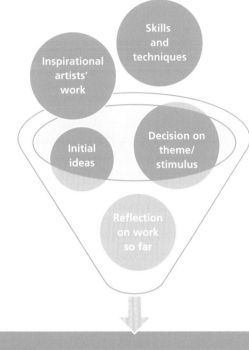

Skills and techniques

Inspirational artists' work

Initial ideas

Decision on theme/stimulus

Reflection on work so far

**Portfolio**

**Theme/Stimulus**

**Investigation studies/images**

**Compositional developments and exploration of techniques relating to one idea**

**Final piece**

**Evaluation**

**Presentation of portfolio for external assessment**

**Assessment**

40 marks are available for showing your creative process

50 marks are available for demonstrating expressive skills

10 marks are available for the evaluation

Your finished portfolio is sent to SQA for external assessment

## National 4

Your work does not need to be sent to SQA for external assessment so you do not need to present it as a portfolio. Your teacher will advise you on what format your work should be for internal assessment.

Your final outcome is an important part of your added value unit, which you need to complete to achieve your course award.

Use the checklist on this page to help you keep track of your expressive portfolio and to ensure that you meet the assessment standards. For submission to SQA, you may find that your teacher will help you with the presentation or labelling of your portfolio, or you may be required to do this by yourself.

| | Task | Success criteria | ✓ |
|---|---|---|---|
| **EXPRESSIVE PORTFOLIO CHECKLIST** | | | |
| 1 | Theme/stimulus | I have selected a theme/title/stimulus. | |
| 2 | Investigation and research | I have completed some observational studies of subject matter related to my theme/title/stimulus. | |
| | | I have compiled any other relevant investigative research (e.g. photography, images of an inspirational artist's work). | |
| 3 | Development | I have selected one idea for development. | |
| | | I have completed compositional developments based on my idea which are appropriate to my theme/title/stimulus. | |
| | | My development studies show that I have explored appropriate materials and techniques. | |
| | | My development studies link well visually to my investigation work. | |
| 4 | Final piece | I have planned my final outcome, deciding on the most appropriate composition, scale, materials and technique. | |
| | | I have ensured that my final piece has further refinement from my development (e.g. improvements in composition, lighting, technique). | |
| | | I have produced my outcome to the best standard I am capable of. | |
| | | If appropriate (for 3D work only), I have photographed my outcome, or arranged for it to be photographed. | |
| 5 | Evaluation | I have completed my evaluation on the appropriate SQA template. | |
| | | I have evaluated the effectiveness of my creative process by giving justified personal opinions on the decisions I made when working through my portfolio. | |
| | | I have given justified personal opinions on the effectiveness of the visual qualities of my portfolio, referring to my theme/stimulus. | |
| 6 | Portfolio presentation | I have discussed the most suitable presentation format with my teacher, considering shape and size of card/paper. | |
| | | I have included my title/theme/stimulus on the first sheet. | |
| | | I have included my evaluation on the first sheet. | |
| | | I have selected relevant investigation work which all links visually with my final piece. | |
| | | I have selected relevant development work which shows one line of development and which all links visually with my investigation and final piece. | |
| | | I have arranged my work into a suitable layout, so that my creative process is clear, and discussed this with my teacher before proceeding. | |
| | | I have not exceeded the maximum 3 × A2 sheets (or equivalent). | |
| | | I have carefully and neatly stuck down my work, including my final piece (or photographs of my final piece if it is 3D). | |
| | | The separate sheets of my portfolio have been securely taped together on the back. | |
| | | The correct labels supplied by SQA have been stuck onto the back of my portfolio. | |
| | Well done – you've made it! | | |

# 'Flotsam & jetsam'

## STILL LIFE CASE STUDY

**2**

- Investigation and research
- Creating compositions
- Using technology
- Expressive art studies
- Development studies
- Artistic influences
- Final piece

# Investigation and research

Emily's teacher had a selection of still life themes for her to choose from. The theme that appealed to her most was 'Flotsam & Jetsam'. At this stage, Emily began exploring observational drawing and media handling techniques. Emily drew a variety of objects relating to her theme. Emily's teacher encouraged her to work from primary source materials (drawing objects that are in front of you).

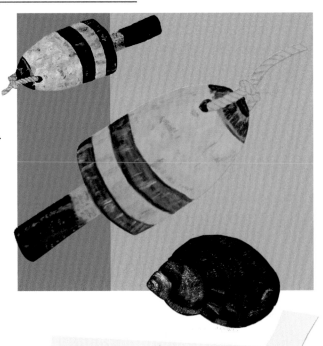

## HINTS & TIPS

Good-quality drawings and paintings are the key to this project. Choose objects that tell a story or fit into your theme. Pick different sizes of objects and use a variety of heights, shapes, forms, textures and colours.

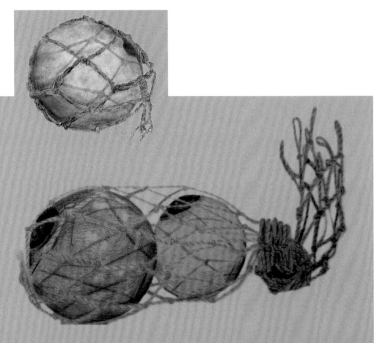

Emily began exploring her preferred techniques: acrylic paint, watercolour and coloured pencil. Her confidence increased as she developed these techniques. She began to really enjoy painting and wanted to develop this further in her portfolio.

# Creating compositions

To develop compositional ideas, Emily began by using a viewfinder and her camera. She positioned the objects into an interesting composition. By using her camera, she found it easier to experiment with unusual viewpoints.

Emily tried out a variety of compositions. She photographed the objects from above, which she did not like. She then cropped an image to create a square format. Emily liked the yellow lantern with the red reflector as her focal point.

## HINTS & TIPS

To create compositional ideas, use a viewfinder or your camera's screen. Isolate the key elements in a scene and check their placement using the viewfinder. This makes it easier to compose your objects. Consider the number of objects in your composition. An odd number of elements will usually look better than an even number.

Emily varied her compositional studies and placed the objects with a strong horizontal emphasis. The bottle created a vertical focal point on the right-hand side of the image. Emily experimented further and created a more balanced composition by placing the bottle centrally.

Emily liked the vertical emphasis of the bottle and decided to explore this in one of her compositional studies.

Emily zoomed in to an area to create impact. Cropping objects helps to create tension but also focuses attention on certain areas of the composition. Emily considered how the objects were spaced, varying the space between the elements in her composition. Overlapping objects can create a busy and interesting composition.

# Using technology

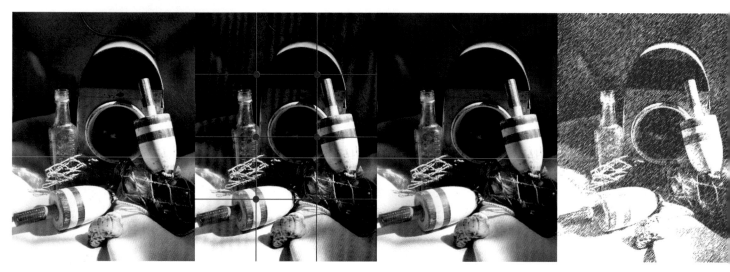

## COMMON MISTAKES

Photography is a great way to develop compositional ideas. However, sometimes students are tempted to copy their photographs using tracing paper or a light box, or even to work over photocopies of the images with media. This is very obvious to markers. If you do this in your expressive portfolio, it will affect your mark as you are not demonstrating that you have met the assessment standards – you are required to show skill in observational drawing and media handling.

Emily began exploring one particular photograph by using digital imaging software. She found that she could quickly create changes. She decided to produce some thumbnails after this exercise to help with her expressive development.

### The focal point

The focal point of a painting is what draws the viewer's eye to it. It is usually the main aspect you first notice when you look at the composition.

### The Rule of Thirds

You can place your objects on the 'intersection points' from a Rule of Thirds grid. Check that the objects in the painting lead the eye towards the focal point.

### Is there variety?

Try not to use the same type of composition all the time, no matter how successful it is. Vary where you put the horizon line, where you put the focal point and swap between portrait and landscape format compositions.

## HINTS & TIPS

Remember to photograph your compositions from different viewpoints. Try zooming into a composition to create unusual development studies. It is important to create balance. Experiment with objects of different sizes and consider the effect of colour.

# Expressive art studies

*Le Vase Paille* (1895) by Paul Cézanne

Emily studied a variety of still life artists in her expressive art studies. She took inspiration from Paul Cézanne because she found that his technique was particularly relevant to how she painted. She liked his use of visible brushwork and, after investigating his techniques, she concentrated on using expressive brushwork to emphasise the form of the objects. Emily found that Cézanne's subject matter was not particularly relevant to her own work but she liked his use of colour. Cézanne's muted colour palette with emphasis on applying and blending his colours with small brushstrokes inspired Emily.

*Still Life with Seven Apples* (1878) by Paul Cézanne

*Shelves of Fruit* (1995) by Leon Morrocco

Emily loved Leon Morrocco's work but knew that his strong vibrant colour palette did not suit her own work. She decided to experiment with his techniques of framing still life compositions with a seascape. She also liked how he would often compose objects on a shelf and use patterned fabric to provide a vertical emphasis.

# Development studies

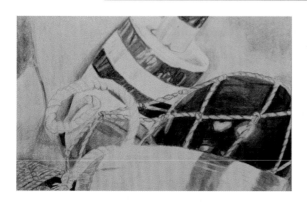

After completing some quick development studies in her sketchbook, Emily decided on the choice of objects for her portfolio developments. She loved the ship's lantern and wanted this to be one of her main objects. She had some issues with all the other objects being smaller in comparison to the lantern. Her teacher advised her to include the wooden floats to allow for a more dynamic composition.

## HINTS & TIPS

Develop thumbnails of your compositions. Thumbnails are small-scale sketches which quickly allow you to see a variety of viewpoints, create different focal points and see how objects relate to each other in terms of scale and colour.

Emily loved the result of this painted composition. The brushwork and depth of colour was strong. Cézanne's influence can be clearly seen. She took the advice of her teacher not to be scared of applying more colours through layers of paint. You can see Emily's confidence increasing in her compositional studies.

# Artistic influences

In her sketchbook, Emily completed a number of small thumbnail studies exploring different seascapes which could be used as her background. She eventually decided to use a dark stormy seascape. Emily decided that the range of tonal blues would enhance the yellow of the ship's lantern. The warm and cold colour contrast will create a dynamic final composition.

*Still Life looking towards Stromboli and Panarea* by Leon Morrocco

'I am really interested in Morrocco's background seascape, which contrasts with the still life objects in the foreground. I think I will try to complete some development studies to see if this would work in my painting. Morrocco used warm and cold colours in many of his studies. The cold colours help the background to recede and the warm coloured objects appear to come closer to the viewer.'

# Final piece

## NATIONAL 5 ART AND DESIGN – EXPRESSIVE PORTFOLIO EVALUATION

| Candidate name: | Emily | Candidate number: | 000000 |
|---|---|---|---|
| Centre number: | | 000000 | |

**Instructions to candidates**

You should reflect on and critically evaluate the creative process you followed when working through your expressive portfolio. In your evaluation give justified personal opinions on:
- the decisions you made when working through your portfolio
- the effectiveness of the visual qualities of your portfolio, referring to your theme/stimulus.

**10 marks**

- I explored different compositions by rearranging my objects in different ways. Sometimes, I would remove an object to see what difference this made, especially the lamp which was quite a dominant object because of the yellow colour and the scale of it. In the end, I made the decision to include it in my final piece as it gave a burst of colour and contrasted with the dark background.
- I tried different viewpoints including views from above and a cropped view, but I felt the eye-level viewpoints and views from slightly above the objects allowed me to experiment more with background which was an important feature of Leon Morrocco's work, who was my inspirational artist.
- I experimented with a number of materials and I felt that the acrylic paint technique that I had used in my development was definitely my most successful media handling technique as the intensity of the colour gave good visual impact. This gave me the confidence to use this technique in my final piece.
- As I was completing my development, I decided that I would place a seascape in the background rather than have the objects look like they were lying on the sand. I spent a long time finding an appropriate image to include in my investigation, which I painted separately at first and this allowed me to practise my technique.
- I am really pleased with the effect of the seascape in my still life composition. The influence of Morrocco can be clearly seen here as he also used the sea and sky as a background at times. I feel that it contrasts well with the foreground of my painting.
- The stormy clouds in the sky are different from Morrocco's backgrounds as he worked around the Mediterranean and usually has bright blue skies. In my painting, the dark sky creates a dramatic mood and atmosphere which I thought was more appropriate for Scotland.
- I really like the concrete wall which my objects sat on. I added this as a further improvement in my final piece. I painted it with colours which would harmonise with the objects. This detail makes my still life more interesting as it helps to suggest a particular place.
- I am especially pleased with my expressive brushwork which adds form and texture to the objects and gives a strong atmospheric quality to my painting.
- One of the things I would like to have achieved, but struggled a bit with, was the distorted perspective in Morrocco's work. I found it hard to move away from a more realistic perspective and felt it would have been a bit of a risk for me. I think I would need more practice with this type of work before I was confident enough.
- I think my final piece successfully reflects my theme of 'Flotsam & Jetsam' as the objects are all things which might be found washed up on a beach and the sea in the background also communicates this idea.

# 'Dulce et decorum est'

**2**

- Investigation and research
- Expressive art studies
- Development of narrative
- Composition and media handling
- Final piece

# Investigation and research

Beth decided to work with a title and a narrative to develop her expressive activity. She loved history and was especially interested in the First World War. She was keen to explore a more emotional response to this theme.

First, Beth explored several possible titles using key phrases to help her with her creative development. She found war quotations and phrases which inspired her initial development:

- World War I
- Chemical warfare
- War games
- Peace versus war
- Conflict
- Gassing
- Bio hazard

She explored each of these titles, mainly through spidergrams and thumbnail sketches. Her breakthrough came when she researched war literature and poetry. Discovering the poem *Dulce et Decorum Est* by Wilfred Owen became a pivotal moment in her expressive activity. She analysed the poem and picked out this particular verse:

*Gas! Gas! Quick, boys! — An ecstasy of fumbling,*
*Fitting the clumsy helmets just in time;*
*But someone still was yelling out and stumbling,*
*And flound'ring like a man in fire or lime …*
*Dim, through the misty panes and thick green light,*
*As under a green sea, I saw him drowning.*

Beth's drawing of a gas mask using the medium of coloured pencils was very successful due to the strength of application. She also enjoyed painting the skull. This image was to become a key element in later development studies, with the skull being explored in a variety of media and techniques.

# Expressive art studies

*Pipe, Glass, Bottle of Vieux Marc* (1914) by Pablo Picasso

Beth spent time studying art that portrays war. She looked at war artists through posters, photography and painting.

Beth became increasingly interested in the technique of collage because she wanted to incorporate text with an image. She researched where collage had been used in expressive art and found that Picasso had used printed text in his paintings during his Cubist period. He used this technique to enhance the meaning of his still life works.

*Weeping Woman* (1937) by Pablo Picasso

*The Troubled City* (1991) by Ken Currie

After further research she also found that Picasso had completed a series of paintings depicting the horrors of the Spanish Civil War. The painting *Weeping Woman* (1937) particularly inspired Beth. The emotion conveyed by a woman crying appealed to Beth, and the green hues used by Picasso gave her the confidence to try her own version, which was more realistic but conveyed a symbolic message through the use of colour.

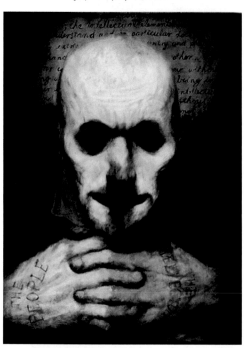

*Head of an Idealist* (1990) by Ken Currie

Ken Currie was the second artist Beth investigated. Beth found his war paintings difficult to look at because of the scenes of civil unrest that Currie depicted. In one painting, the figures were burning books and beating up men. It reminded Beth of television footage she had seen. She could relate to the subject matter that Currie had portrayed and liked the dark, sombre tones of his paintings.

Beth studied further work by Currie and found his later portraiture work really inspiring. *Head of an Idealist* was one of her favourites because of the skeletal face, which reminded her of her own skull study. Currie had also used text in the background, and Beth found the tattooed hands reinforced the message of the painting. This portrait had a luminous quality about it through Currie's dramatic use of light. The colour palette was limited, using muted dark, earthy tones which gave the portrait a sinister quality.

# Development of theme

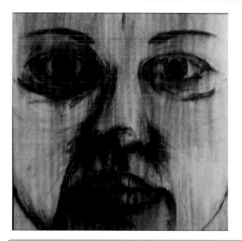

Beth decided her main focus would be the emotional aspect of war and particularly the gassing incident described in the poem. She used a pen and wash technique in her thumbnail portrait and then tried an emotional pose to convey the effects of war. Some of these studies remained in her sketchbook and were not developed further in her portfolio.

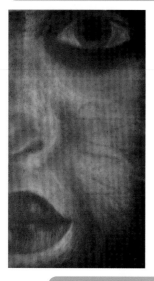

### Teacher's feedback

Beth, your observational drawings and paintings are excellent. I like the thumbnail compositions. The study of half your face combined with the skull demonstrates how difficult it is to achieve a realistic appearance. You seem to have lost the language and narrative evident in your earlier work. I would advise you to start incorporating text into your next developments.

At this point, Beth began to experiment with text-based art, in which she had previously expressed an interest in her expressive art studies.

Incorporating text into her work became one of Beth's main techniques. In her expressive art studies she had looked at collage and the Cubists. She began to use their technique of incorporating related language to help explain the painting. This was particularly successful in the gas mask composition.

# Composition and media handling

Beth explored a variety of media techniques. She worked on prepared grounds, which included marbled paper, and used paint, pen and wash, collage, coloured pencil and oil pastel. She decided she wanted to use a mixed-media approach in her final piece.

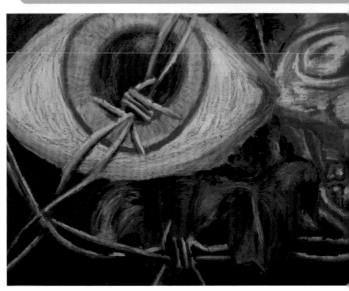

Beth developed many of her compositions by zooming in and cropping sketches that were originally larger to focus in on key areas. She used a viewfinder to help her with this approach.

She spent time exploring the skull, which symbolised death, and kept her main colour palette to a range of muted greens. The green colour palette symbolised the poem's lines, 'And flound'ring like a man in fire or lime ... Dim, through the misty panes and thick green light.' She found that by using the complementary colour of red, it enhanced the green tones and also represented the word fire.

# Final piece

## NATIONAL 5 ART AND DESIGN – EXPRESSIVE PORTFOLIO EVALUATION

| Candidate name: | Beth | Candidate number: | 000000 |
| --- | --- | --- | --- |
| Centre number: | | 000000 | |

**Instructions to candidates**

You should reflect on and critically evaluate the creative process you followed when working through your expressive portfolio. In your evaluation give justified personal opinions on:
- the decisions you made when working through your portfolio
- the effectiveness of the visual qualities of your portfolio, referring to your theme/stimulus.

**10 marks**

- When I selected my theme 'Dulce et Decorum Est' I had a lot of ideas in my head about how I could develop it. I decided on a mixed-media approach as I had been looking at Picasso's synthetic Cubism in class and liked the way he combined painting with collage and text.
- I wanted to do something experimental for my portfolio. I feel that I achieved this with my technique. I am pleased with my visual interpretation of the poem by Wilfred Owen, and how I used certain objects, such as the skull and gas mask, to show the horror of war.
- When I was working on composition, I decided to always include the skull, gas mask or both. I also tried including barbed wire in a couple of developments. I experimented with including elements of my own face and tried cropped views and close-ups. In the end, I thought it was more effective to use my face like a traditional portrait but to add the other elements in the background, as if they were thoughts going on in my head.
- I am pleased with my colour palette of red and green which symbolised the chlorine gas and fire. As my development went on, I decided this limited palette was the most effective so that all the elements were connected by this.
- I decided to include text in my work and it was quite easy to find suitable words in newspapers and magazines because a lot of headlines are still about war and disasters, which shows not much has changed.
- When I was completing my development I tried some print-making and I liked the graphic effect this gave. I found it difficult to decide between this technique and painting. I chose what I most enjoyed, which was the mixed-media painting technique.
- I love the background of newsprint, paint and stencilling. These were techniques I tried in my investigation and development. Combining them gave a result better than I expected and I like the combination of images and words.
- If I was completing this piece again, I would like to improve the proportions of the face. I don't feel as if they are quite right, although the distortion does add to the nightmarish mood and atmosphere.
- I find my self-portrait difficult to evaluate because it is me, but I am pleased with the painting techniques I developed in my portfolio. I achieved my aim of producing an expressive and experimental piece of work combining expressive painting techniques with collage.
- I feel that my final piece communicates the theme of 'Dulce et Decorum Est' as it portrays the horror of the poem in a creative way with the portrait and the overlapping image in the background which look like flashbacks. As I chose a piece of literature as a theme, I also think the use of text is appropriate.

# EXPRESSIVE MEDIA TECHNIQUES

**2**

- Tonal studies
- Paints
- Coloured pencils
- Tonal printmaking and charcoal
- Chalk and collage
- Drawing techniques
- Printmaking, batik and oil pastels
- Mixed media and 3D low relief
- Ceramics

# Tonal studies

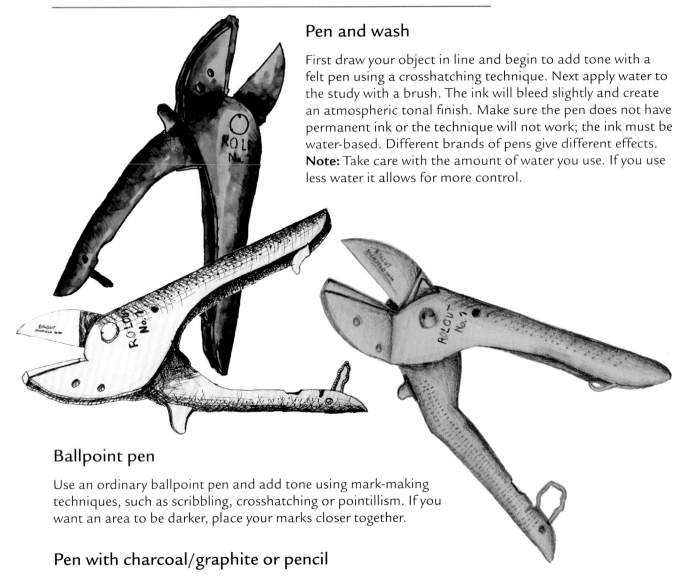

## Pen and wash

First draw your object in line and begin to add tone with a felt pen using a crosshatching technique. Next apply water to the study with a brush. The ink will bleed slightly and create an atmospheric tonal finish. Make sure the pen does not have permanent ink or the technique will not work; the ink must be water-based. Different brands of pens give different effects. **Note:** Take care with the amount of water you use. If you use less water it allows for more control.

## Ballpoint pen

Use an ordinary ballpoint pen and add tone using mark-making techniques, such as scribbling, crosshatching or pointillism. If you want an area to be darker, place your marks closer together.

## Pen with charcoal/graphite or pencil

These are the most commonly used media for tonal studies. It is important for your drawing to have a range of tonal values – light, medium and dark.

## Pen with watercolour wash

Begin your study using an ordinary ballpoint pen and then apply a wash of watercolour paint. This should be a light wash of paint (watery), not thick paint, or you will cover your drawing.

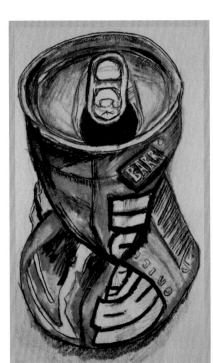

## Coloured ballpoint pen

Try blue ballpoint pen worked over with watercolour for another variation using this technique.

# Paints

Watercolour, gouache, acrylics, tempera paste and tempera blocks are all paints commonly used in schools. Each type of paint gives a different effect. It is only through experimentation that you can see which medium you prefer. Watercolour usually gives a subtle and delicate transparent finish. Gouache and tempera paste can be in tubes, tubs or in blocks and is similar to a water-based paint like watercolour, but can be applied more thickly and is often opaque. Acrylic paint can be applied either opaquely or with a transparent wash. It dries very quickly and is excellent for creating strong, expressive brush marks. Although acrylic is water-based, it becomes permanent when dry, so can be overworked without the colours underneath bleeding through.

There are a number of different painting techniques. You can work wet on wet to blend colours, or use dry brushwork (lightly brushing wet paint over dry paint) to create a dramatic effect. This technique is great for applying highlights and detail to your painting.

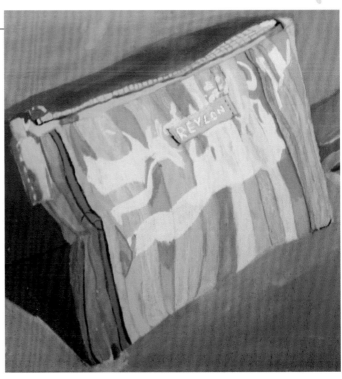

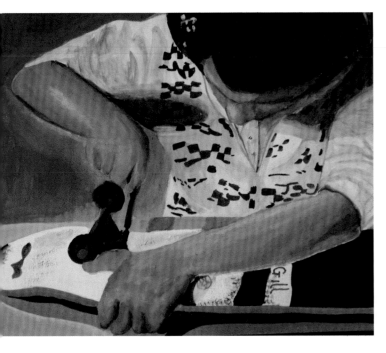

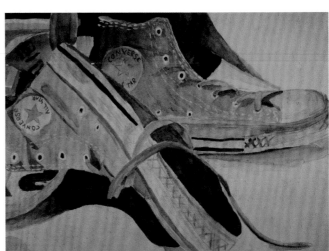

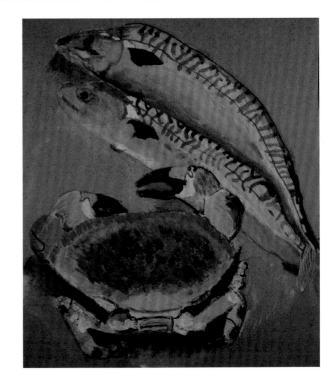

## HINTS & TIPS

Using different qualities of paper with the same media can create very different outcomes. So if you like a certain medium, such as coloured pencil, try different papers, such as textured paper, brown or black paper, coloured or prepared papers.

# Coloured pencils

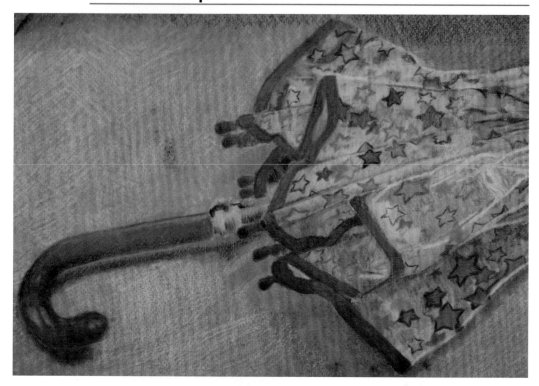

Coloured pencils are a good medium to use as they are quick and easy to learn to use well. They are also a versatile medium and can be used to enhance other media such as paint.

Shade the area carefully and build up the tones gradually. It is important to apply the colour slowly but strongly. Aim to capture contrasts of dark and light. The direction of your pencil marks will help to suggest form.

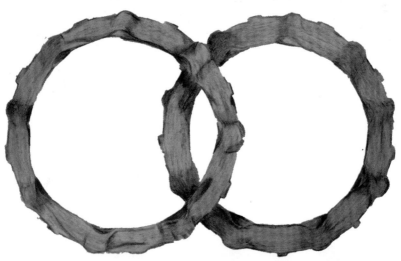

Artist-quality soft coloured pencils are good for blending colours together. You can overlay a variety of different colours to give a drawing depth. Different techniques you can use include cross hatching, shading and overlaying.

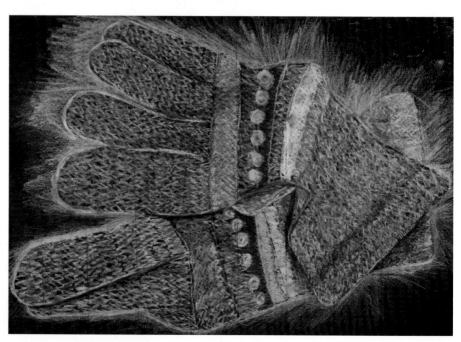

# Tonal printmaking and charcoal

## Polyprint

This is an unusual technique which can give quick results. Take a prepared polyprint block onto which you have already transferred a line drawing. Instead of rolling on the ink, paint onto the block with the printing ink instead. You need to use block printing ink, which will not dry out as you are working. Use black and white or shades and tints of one colour. For best results print on slightly damp, stretched paper. You will need to blot your print with scrap paper to remove any excess ink.

## HINTS & TIPS

The brown paper background gives this white, grey and black coloured pencil study a different quality. A range of tonal values (dark, medium and light tones) have been used to make the objects appear 3D.

## Charcoal

Charcoal is a medium which can be used to create strong tonal contrast. This drawing medium is expressive and can also be used with chalk pastel to highlight or add a hint of colour. Charcoal studies can be created by using your rubber as a drawing tool to rub in highlights.

# Chalk and collage

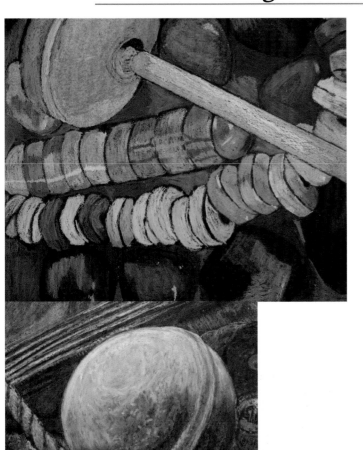

## Chalk pastels

Chalk pastels are soft colour pigments compressed into a stick. You can use chalk in a controlled mark-making technique on its own, or use pastels over paint to add emphasis or highlights. Chalk pastels can be easily blended and are very versatile, and can be used to create a subtle effect or for a more expressive mark-making technique. Pastels should be used on a coloured or black background to achieve the best results. They work best on slightly textured, rough paper.

## Collage

Get some magazines and tear out some images that have the same colours and tones as your subject. Tear or cut these pictures into small pieces and glue them in a mosaic-like technique, matching the colours and tones to create your own image.

# Drawing techniques

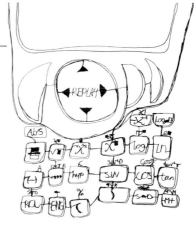

## Continuous line drawing

Continuous line is a great method of producing drawings which have a lovely fresh quality. The technique is simple: take a pen and keep it in contact with the paper until you have completed the entire drawing. It is also a very good way of improving your observational skills.

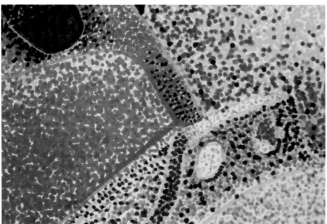

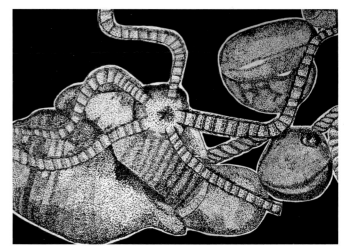

## Pointillism

Pointillism is a well-known technique which can be used with a variety of media. The technique is very simple to achieve. You can use a pen, oil pastel or paint brush to build up the dots. Darker tones are achieved by placing the dots closer together. You can also use a thicker pen to create the darker areas or block in very dark areas entirely.

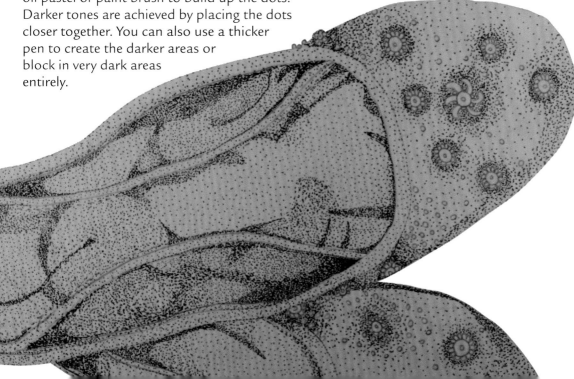

# Printmaking, batik and oil pastels

## Printmaking

Printmaking is a versatile approach to produce a different type of development study or a final outcome. The main types of printmaking used in schools are monoprint, polyprint, lino cut and block print.

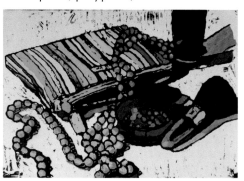

## Paper batik

Paper batik is an unusual technique which can produce interesting results. Make a line drawing in pencil on white cartridge. Go over your pencil lines heavily with chalk. Use tempera paste which has been mixed to a thick and creamy consistency to paint inside the chalk lines. If you mix the colours with white paint to produce tints, it tends to give you more reliable results. Allow the painting to dry overnight and then test a separate small sample by painting over with waterproof ink. Some brands of ink are not effective and you will not want to ruin your work!

Place your finished inked painting on a drawing board in the sink and gently wash off with running water. A watering can is a good idea as it is gentle enough not to wash away your entire painting. Be patient with the washing-off stage. If there are any stubborn areas, rub very gently with a small sponge. You will gradually see your painting revealed.

## Oil pastels

Oil pastel is a versatile and quick medium. You can use a dotted pointillism technique or small linear marks to create a range of tonal values. You can also create highlights and texture by using a cocktail stick to remove some of the oil pastel and reveal the colour underneath.

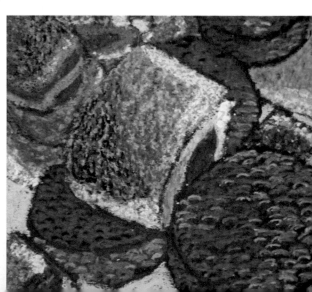

# Mixed media and 3D low relief

## Mixed media

Mixed media can be very effective in altering a painting or drawing that is not working. You have nothing to lose by adding another layer of media to an image that is not successful. By adding a textural technique over an existing painting, you can enhance the painting and give it depth or atmosphere.

## Texture

Texture in painting can be created by adding materials such as sand, wood shavings or eggshells to PVA glue. This mixture can be added to the surface and painted over. This 3D effect creates texture.

Form can be suggested by building up areas of the work with layers of corrugated card. This technique works best if you apply a layer of tissue paper all over before you start painting to tidy and blend in the edges.

Gluing layers of tissue paper to the surface before you start painting can add another quality to your work. Gesso (a type of primer used by artists) can also be used to add textural effects before you start to paint.

# Ceramics

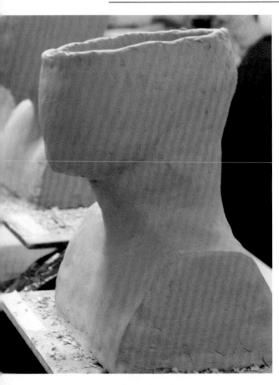

Ceramics can be a great method of expressing yourself three dimensionally. Make sure your art and design department has a kiln and clay facilities before you decide to develop a ceramic project. Some schools specialise in this type of work and have teachers with a lot of knowledge in this area.

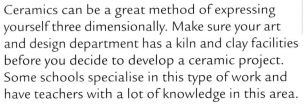

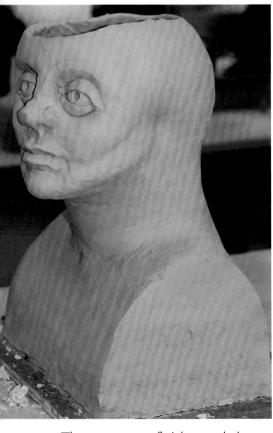

There are various methods that you can use to produce work in clay, from coils, slab work and low relief to other ceramic-media handling techniques. It requires a certain amount of specialist knowledge and planning. There are health and safety issues regarding the use of clay which your classroom teacher can advise on.

There are many finishes and glazes that you can use to achieve an interesting finish to your work. Iron oxide is a simple finish that helps to bring out the texture of the work, but you can also use acrylic paint. All-over colour effects tend to work best.

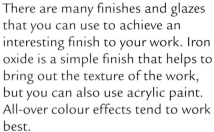

Chapter 3

# 3 Design Activity

---

## Introduction and overview

### What is design?

Design is about solving a problem, about planning how something will look and function, and how it will be made. It is about meeting the needs of a client or target market.

### What will I be doing in this activity?

You will be producing a **portfolio** of design work in response to a **design brief**.

You will work within a particular design area:

> **GRAPHICS**
> or
> **PRODUCT DESIGN**
> or
> **ARCHITECTURAL/ENVIRONMENTAL/INTERIOR DESIGN**
> or
> **JEWELLERY**
> or
> **FASHION/TEXTILES**

**NOTE:** Your teacher may not offer you a choice or may offer you a limited choice. This is because departments often specialise in one or two areas which they have the expertise, equipment and resources to deliver. This ensures that you get the support and resources you need to complete the project.

You will also complete some **design studies** work. This should be related to the design area you have selected. The design studies tasks will help you to understand the key issues in your chosen design area.

# The design process

In your design activity, you will be following a **design process**:

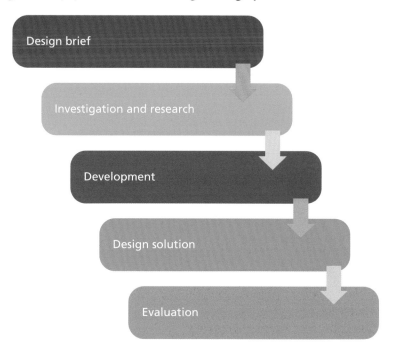

# Your design brief

The design process is essentially a problem-solving activity, which you complete step by step. The first step is the design brief, which gives you information on requirements and constraints (restrictions). Your brief should be specific enough to give you the information you need but open-ended enough to allow you to be creative.

Your brief should contain information on:

**HINTS & TIPS**

It is worthwhile spending time getting your design brief right as it will make a difference to the success of the activity as a whole.

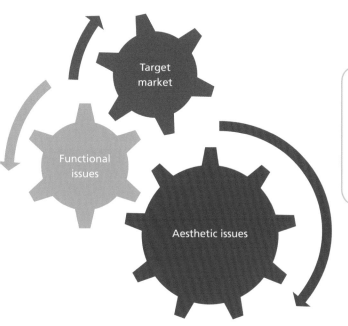

## National 4

You will follow a similar design process to National 5 candidates. However, the development of the selected idea at National 5 level requires more in-depth exploration.

## Writing your brief

Your teacher may give you a design brief, and this is acceptable, but you may be asked to generate your own, or to adapt a basic brief.

Here are some examples to help you to understand what makes an effective design brief:

| GRAPHIC DESIGN |
| --- |
| Design a poster for a music festival.<br>                    Far too open-ended – there isn't enough information. |
| Design a poster. It should contain an image of a piano and Art Deco style lettering.<br>                    Too restrictive! |
| Design a poster for a music festival. The festival will feature jazz music and your design should communicate this through your choice of imagery, lettering, layout, colour and style.<br><br>The festival will take place at Strathclyde Park on 14th July, starting at 2.30 p.m.<br>                    Much better! |
| **JEWELLERY DESIGN** |
| Design a piece of jewellery based on nature.<br>                    Too open-ended – where would you begin? |
| Design a brooch which looks like a flower. It should appeal to teenage girls so the colour should be pink.<br>                    No scope for creativity. |
| You have been commissioned to design a piece of statement jewellery. The client is in her mid-20s and is a collector of unusual jewellery. Her style is theatrical and unorthodox and your jewellery design should demonstrate this.<br><br>The piece should be a large-scale brooch, inspired by sea creatures. Your choice of materials and colour scheme should reflect the inspiration.<br><br>The piece should be durable enough for special-occasion wear and you should consider suitable fastenings.<br>                    Scope to be creative and plenty of information. Well done! |

## HINTS & TIPS

Ensure that your design brief is realistic and achievable. For instance, it might be unrealistic to say that you will design a prom dress if you have no experience of sewing and garment construction, and have a limited budget.

## Successful designers are:

### Curious

You should explore all the aspects of your design brief. What are you being asked to do? What do you need to find out? Then go and investigate!

### Open-minded

Don't be too fixed in your thinking. Be willing to change your mind depending on what you discover and how your ideas develop.

### Creative and imaginative

In the early stages, it is important to come up with several ideas. This is often difficult for young designers. You may find that you have a fixed idea about what your design solution will look like. Remember, you haven't been through the design process yet and you are unlikely to have come up with your best idea at the start.

### Not afraid to take risks

It is a fact that you will learn more from what doesn't work than from your successes, so never be afraid to experiment and try things. This is particularly important in the first stages of the project.

### Determined

At times, you will feel like you're 'stuck'. This is normal! If you work through this, you will be at your most creative. Try to approach the problem from different angles. Try a new technique. Try rearranging a design. Try making things bigger, smaller, whatever. It is important to keep going and you will suddenly find that you have come up with new, and probably better, solutions.

### Good at taking advice

Think about your teacher as representing your 'client'. It's their job to make suggestions, to point out what's not working, to tell you if you're not fulfilling the original brief. Take this feedback positively. This is how real designers find out what they need to know to refine their ideas.

### Good at meeting deadlines

Your work is submitted for external assessment, so you have to finish it on time! It is important to meet all of the interim deadlines set by your teacher, as well as the final deadline, otherwise you will run out of time and may not be able to finish your final outcome to the best standard, which will affect your mark.

### Good at making judgements and decisions

It is really important that you choose your best initial idea to develop for the portfolio as this will be the work that your mark is derived from.

## HINTS & TIPS

Good time management is key to the success of this activity. If you miss one interim deadline, this may have a knock-on effect on the rest of your project. You may find that you have to rush to finish at the end.

## Investigation and research

This is the part of the process where you should be thinking about what you need to find out to solve your design problem successfully. If you have produced an effective design brief, this will give you some clues about what you need to investigate.

At this point, it's worth spending some time planning what you are going to do. The following diagram should give you some ideas:

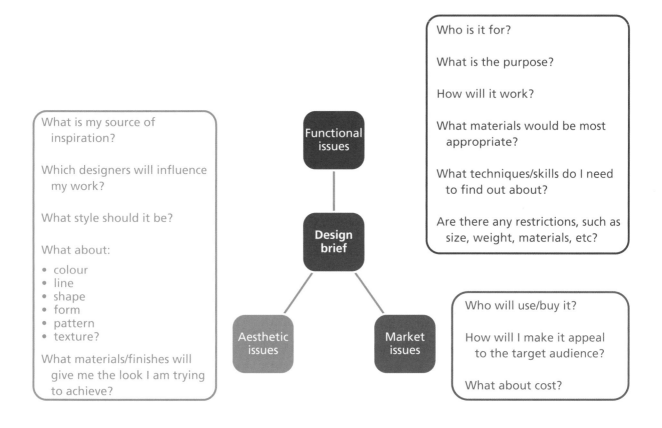

What is my source of inspiration?

Which designers will influence my work?

What style should it be?

What about:

- colour
- line
- shape
- form
- pattern
- texture?

What materials/finishes will give me the look I am trying to achieve?

**Functional issues**

**Design brief**

**Aesthetic issues**

**Market issues**

Who is it for?

What is the purpose?

How will it work?

What materials would be most appropriate?

What techniques/skills do I need to find out about?

Are there any restrictions, such as size, weight, materials, etc?

Who will use/buy it?

How will I make it appeal to the target audience?

What about cost?

How will I present my investigation and research visually to show evidence of what I have done? Consider:

- images – photos/cuttings/print-outs
- personal drawing
- samples of materials/techniques
- examples of designers' work
- market research
- information
- annotation

Where will I find what I need?

## HINTS & TIPS

It is important to move on to development as soon as you have enough research material. Most people spend far too long on research as it can be very enjoyable!

# Development

This stage of the process is where you create your own ideas in response to the brief. It is best to tackle this in three stages:

| Initial ideas | • Consider a number of different possibilities – remember to work from your investigation and research material<br>• Generate rough ideas – these can be drawings or 3D mock-ups or samples |
| --- | --- |

| Selection of best idea | • Evaluate work done so far to see which idea is the best – remember to refer to your brief<br>• Select the best idea for development |
| --- | --- |

| Development and refinement of selected idea | • Experiment with changes<br>• Explore techniques and materials<br>• Refine the idea to make improvements – reflect on your brief as you work to make sure you stay on track |
| --- | --- |

# Design solution

Your design solution should show your finished concept. Although you are not expected to achieve a professional finish at this level, you should aim for the best quality possible so that your idea is communicated clearly.

A poorly executed outcome will affect your final mark, so it is worthwhile taking time to plan and to select appropriate materials. You do not need to use expensive materials or processes, but if resources are very limited you should consider this at the design brief stage. This will ensure that you don't attempt something that you don't have the resources or level of skill to carry out successfully.

## HINTS & TIPS

In 3D design projects, it is good practice to show some 3D development. To gain maximum marks, you should produce a carefully made 3D solution or a good-quality illustration showing all the important aspects of the design.

## COMMON MISTAKES

Sometimes in graphic design portfolios, design solutions are just direct copies of one of the developments printed in a bigger format. You should ensure that your outcome shows further improvement and refinement or it will be difficult to award you maximum marks.

## Evaluating design work

The general information given in the section entitled 'Evaluating expressive work' on page 13 also applies here.

## What should I evaluate in my design activity?

> **The design process – effectiveness of decisions made when working through your portfolio**

> **The effectiveness of the aesthetic and functional qualities of your portfolio**

### COMMON MISTAKES

Once students start designing, they often forget what their brief was and end up going off in a different direction. This can cause problems if the portfolio ends up looking confused and lacking coherence, and marks can be lost. Reviewing and evaluating your work against your design brief on a regular basis will avoid this.

Your evaluation **must** be completed on the SQA evaluation template which can be downloaded from their website: www.sqa.org.uk/sqa/47388.html. There is no word count limitation as such, but you cannot exceed the space provided and the font size is locked. Therefore, it is recommended that your comments are very focused and concise.

When completed, your evaluation **must** be attached to the first sheet of your design portfolio.

| BASIC AND DESCRIPTIVE COMMENT | EVALUATIVE COMMENT |
|---|---|
| Autumn leaves were the source of inspiration for my textile design. <br><br> Explain why. | I chose autumn leaves as the source of inspiration for my textile design as I liked the warm colour scheme. I felt the shapes and the patterns would be good to develop for textiles. |
| This is my favourite idea. <br><br> Why? | This idea related best to the aims of my brief and it is the most aesthetically pleasing. I chose to develop it further in my portfolio. |
| My design solution is a bit untidy. <br><br> Why, what happened? | My solution was a bit rushed as I didn't manage my time particularly well at the development stage. In future, I would leave myself more time to finish my work to a higher standard. |
| My solution fulfils the design brief. <br><br> In what way? | The chair is suitable for the target market as the futuristic style would appeal to young city apartment dwellers. It is designed to fit the human body, so would be comfortable. The design is suitable for mass production so this would keep the cost down. The chair can be stacked, which was an important aspect of the brief. |

# How your design activity relates to your portfolio

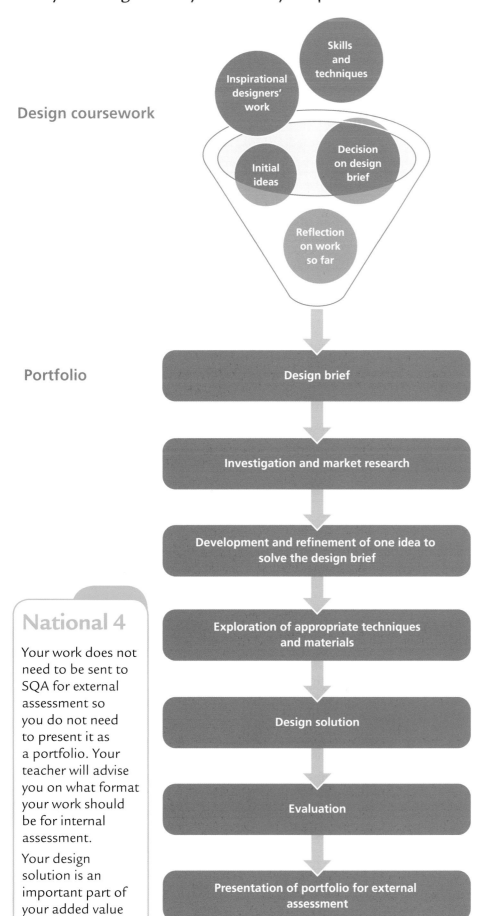

**Design coursework**

- Skills and techniques
- Inspirational designers' work
- Initial ideas
- Decision on design brief
- Reflection on work so far

**Portfolio**

- Design brief
- Investigation and market research
- Development and refinement of one idea to solve the design brief
- Exploration of appropriate techniques and materials
- Design solution
- Evaluation
- Presentation of portfolio for external assessment

**Assessment**

40 marks are available for showing your design process

50 marks are available for demonstrating design skills

10 marks are available for the evaluation

Your finished portfolio is sent to SQA for external assessment

## National 4

Your work does not need to be sent to SQA for external assessment so you do not need to present it as a portfolio. Your teacher will advise you on what format your work should be for internal assessment.

Your design solution is an important part of your added value unit, which you need to complete to achieve your course award.

Use the checklist on this page to help you keep track of your design portfolio and ensure that you meet the assessment standards. You may find that your teacher will help you with the presentation or labelling of your work, or you may be required to do this yourself.

| | Task | Success criteria | ✓ |
|---|---|---|---|
| **DESIGN PORTFOLIO CHECKLIST** | | | |
| 1 | Design brief | My brief is clear and easy to understand. | |
| | | It contains information on the functional issues of the design problem. | |
| | | It gives me direction on aesthetics (look, style, inspiration). | |
| | | It includes information about the target market/audience. | |
| 2 | Investigation and research | I have gathered/produced investigative research on my visual inspiration (e.g. theme/style/source of inspiration) such as drawings and photographs. | |
| | | I have compiled a selection of relevant market research. | |
| | | I have explored the functional aspects of my design brief and gathered any relevant information/material. | |
| 3 | Development | I have selected one idea for development. | |
| | | I have produced a range of developments based on my idea, adapting and refining the idea with reference to the requirements of the brief. | |
| | | I have evidence to show that I have experimented with appropriate materials and techniques, such as samples. | |
| 4 | Design solution | I have planned the production of my solution, taking account of the time, resources and skills required. | |
| | | I have produced my design solution to the best standard I am capable of. | |
| | | For 3D work only, I have photographed my design solution, or arranged for it to be photographed. | |
| 5 | Evaluation | I have completed my evaluation on the appropriate SQA template. | |
| | | I have evaluated the effectiveness of my design process by giving justified personal opinions on the decisions I made when working through my portfolio. | |
| | | I have given justified personal opinions on the effectiveness of the aesthetic and functional qualities of my portfolio, referring to my design brief requirements. | |
| 6 | Portfolio presentation | I have discussed the most suitable presentation format and style with my teacher, considering shape and size of card/paper and colour scheme. | |
| | | I have included my design brief on the first sheet. | |
| | | I have included my evaluation on the first sheet. | |
| | | I have selected relevant investigation work and market research which all links visually with my final piece. | |
| | | I have selected relevant development work which shows one line of development and which all links visually with my investigation and final piece. | |
| | | I have arranged my work into a suitable layout, so that my creative process is clear, and discussed this with my teacher before proceeding. | |
| | | I have not exceeded the maximum 3 × A2 sheets (or equivalent). | |
| | | I have carefully and neatly stuck down my work, including my design solution, or photographs of my design solution (if it is 3D). | |
| | | The separate sheets of my portfolio have been securely taped together on the back. | |
| | | The correct labels supplied by SQA have been stuck onto the back of my portfolio. | |
| **Well done – you've made it!** | | | |

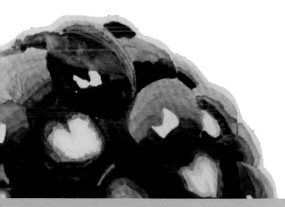

# GRAPHIC DESIGN CASE STUDY

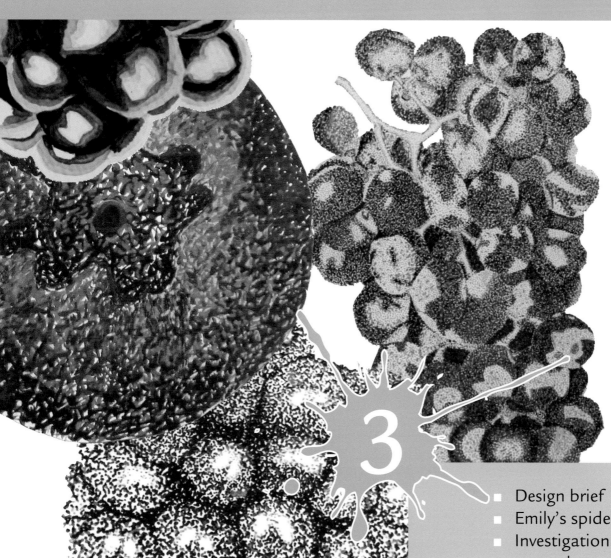

3

# Design brief

Emily has been asked to write a design brief for packaging for a healthy fruit-based drink.

## Emily's first attempt at writing her brief looked like this:

'I am going to design a label which has fruit images on it. I really like cherries. It should be bright and colourful. The target audience is for 5–50 year olds.'

### Teacher's feedback

Good start, Emily. You need to consider a suitable client. You should also consider:

- **Purpose?** Think about this issue.
- **Target Audience/Market?** Health-conscious teenagers and their parents? Where is it to be sold?
- **Who is the client?** A new drinks company?
- **Colour & Style?** This should appeal to your target audience.
- **Imagery?** What sources of inspiration will you use?
- **Text?** Think about appropriate **style** and **size**.
- **Design Requirements?** e.g. bar code, volume capacity.

## HINTS & TIPS

An effective graphic design brief allows you to come up with a range of ideas which will help develop your portfolio of work. You should identify important design issues to help create an interesting solution that answers the problem you have been set. The brief should not be too restrictive or too open-ended.

## Emily's second attempt

'The drinks company "Squeeze" has commissioned me to design packaging for their new range of drinks based on fruit juice. These drinks will be marketed as an alternative to the fizzy drinks bought by teenagers. They are to be sold in supermarkets nationwide.

The packaging will need to appeal to teenagers and their parents and this should be reflected in the colour and style used. Text should be an appropriate font and size.

The imagery used should reflect the ingredients of the product.

I must include the following: bar code and volume capacity.'

### Teacher's feedback

Fantastic! You now have all the information you need to get started.

# Emily's spidergram

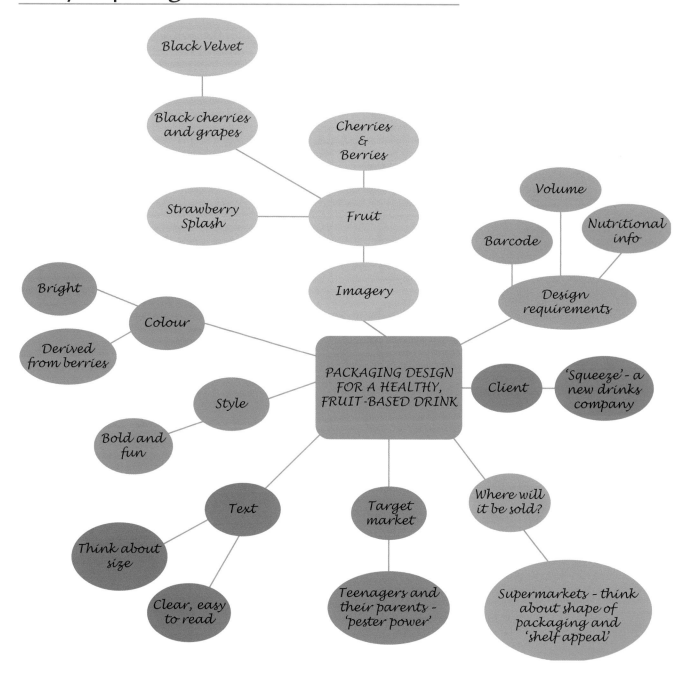

Emily has produced a spidergram to help her sort out the different aspects of her design brief. This has given her some direction for the next stage.

## HINTS & TIPS

Try to be open-minded at this stage. A spidergram should help clarify your thinking, but should not restrict your creativity. If you don't like spidergrams, try writing the information as a list.

# Investigation and research

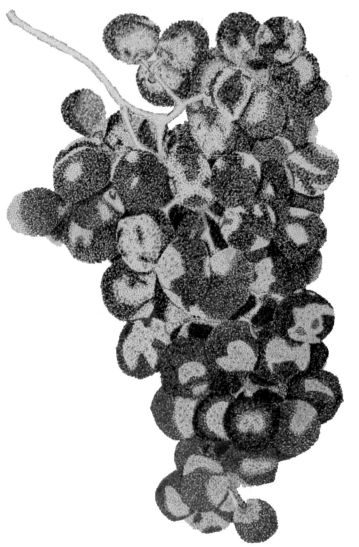

Emily found that the words from her spidergram gave her inspiration and were an important part of the investigation and research process. Emily's school begins with drawings relating to the design brief, so the spidergram gave her direction when she was searching for inspirational images and photographs. She tried to source images which she could develop in her initial ideas.

Emily was told that part of her investigation should be market research. It was important for her to find what was out there in terms of existing products and what contemporary graphic designers were producing. Emily's investigation work gave her the opportunity to explore a whole range of images, market research and techniques.

## How Emily gathered her research

Emily found research materials on the internet, in books, at the library, in magazines and by collecting existing examples of packaging.

She found drawing was also a good method of understanding the visual qualities of her inspirational images and this allowed her to investigate the qualities of line, form, colour, pattern and shape.

## HINTS & TIPS

Although it is not a requirement to produce expressive drawings for your portfolio, it can be very helpful when you are trying to develop original ideas and a personal response to the brief. However, these do not have to be observational studies like you would produce for an expressive portfolio. Drawings for designs have a different purpose.

# Market research

motif

wallpaper

Emily's teacher told her that it was important to explore all options at this stage. The more information that she could find, the more it would help her in the long term to produce interesting ideas.

Emily used the internet to gather market research images. She used a search engine, entering key words related to her brief. She used a variety of different terms. When she found an image she liked Emily clicked on it and viewed it on the actual web page. This meant she could save it as a larger image. It also gave her the opportunity to see the other images available or to follow possible links. When Emily started to exhaust the possibilities with packaging design, she extended her search into related areas such as wallpaper, pattern, motifs and logos.

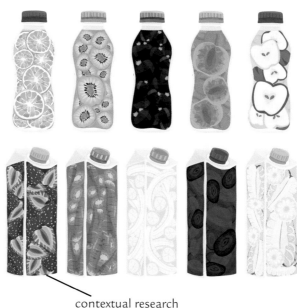

contextual research

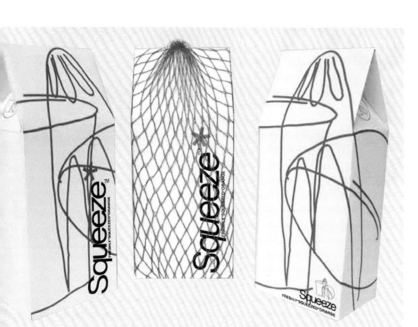

## HINTS & TIPS

Ensure that all of your research is relevant to the design brief.

# Initial ideas

Emily tried different approaches to line drawing. She developed work in her sketchbook by experimenting with a variety of techniques, mixing and matching techniques that she liked. She started simplifying and stylising her images, beginning with simple line drawings of fruit. She then experimented with separating the shapes in her drawings. The quality of Emily's pen work is very precise and she uses a variety of line weights. She experimented with some of the techniques below:

- continuous line drawing
- double line drawing
- positive/negative
- adding pattern
- simplifying the shapes
- repeating the shapes
- overlapping
- zooming in
- changing the colour
- silhouette

## HINTS & TIPS

At this stage, you should begin to produce lots of ideas. Don't worry about how well you draw at this point because it will hinder you in coming up with new ideas. You can always redraw the best concepts later.

Emily decided on a key image to develop further for her portfolio.

'I really loved the circular pattern that I created to represent grapes. This was inspired by the Art Deco poster I researched in my design studies.'

## HINTS & TIPS

To experiment, you can try repeating your motifs. Try a variety of backgrounds and colours. Experiment with different sizes and layouts.

# Design studies

*Pivolo* (1924) by A. M. Cassandre

Emily spent time in her design studies lessons researching graphic designers. She studied the styles and techniques of the designers which related to her own work. She enjoyed this aspect of the course because there were many designers' work she did not select for further study, but which nevertheless helped her develop personal approaches.

Emily decided to study Art Deco design in more depth as she became interested in the geometric shapes typical of this design movement. This inspired her to experiment with simple repeat shapes and to create her own geometric motifs. The limited colour palette of the Art Deco graphic designer A. M. Cassandre inspired her, and she loved his use of bold shapes. She learnt that Cassandre was known for his 'anchoring' technique, which involved connecting the image to the lettering. Emily found this useful in her packaging developments.

## Related designers

**Historical:** This could be from design movements such as Art Nouveau, Art Deco, Bauhaus.

**Contemporary:** There are many young and modern designers.

**Craft:** Often crafts people have a different approach to design, e.g. scrap booking.

## Design studies research

Emily found that her art and design department had an excellent selection of books on graphic design which was helpful for researching designers' work.

*Fruit Store* (1941) Fruit Art Project

*Eat Fruit Be Healthy* (1938)
Fruit Art Project

## Text development

Black Velvet

*Black Velvet*

**Black Velvet**

black velvet

Black Velvet

***BLACK***

***VELVET***

Black Velvet

**Black Velvet**

***Black Velvet***

Black Velvet

**BLACK**

**VELVET**

**HINTS & TIPS**

You can experiment with text using a light box or by taping your work to a window. Trace some of your text in different layouts and styles. You can then add your colour scheme into the letters. You could also try experimenting with pattern.

Emily spent time on the computer experimenting with different fonts. She considered:

- size
- italics
- bold
- font style

She found this way of developing ideas very quick and useful. She experimented with outline fonts, which she filled with her grapes and blackberries designs that she had previously scanned into the computer. She also tried this technique on the light box. Finally, Emily began to incorporate her text ideas and images together.

# Design development

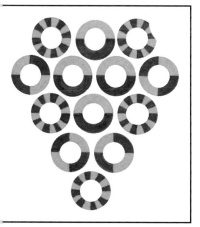

## Teacher's feedback

Look at the negative space around the grapes. Next steps would be to consider zooming into your design and abstracting the grape design further. Start to consider the placement of the lettering.

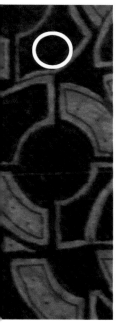

## HINTS & TIPS

Remember to alter the size and shape of your layouts. This may cause problems that you need to solve. For example, *'my text will not fit into that rectangular layout'*. This is a good situation because it forces you to come up with some different possibilities and will help with your design development in the long term. Change is a good thing.

Emily went on to explore her packaging ideas by developing labels for bottles. She decided that the bottle developments were more interesting than the carton format because they were more complicated in shape. She further developed her concept by producing a multi-pack design for holding four bottles of juice.

## Design solution for the portfolio

## NATIONAL 5 ART AND DESIGN – DESIGN PORTFOLIO EVALUATION

| Candidate name: | Emily | Candidate number: | 000000 |
|---|---|---|---|
| Centre number: | 000000 | | |

**Instructions to candidates**

You should reflect on and critically evaluate the creative process you followed when working through your design portfolio. In your evaluation give justified personal opinions on:

- the decisions you made when working through your portfolio
- the effectiveness of the aesthetic and functional qualities of your portfolio, referring to your design brief requirements.

**10 marks**

- In my investigation, I looked at other graphic designers. I particularly liked Cassandre's work from the Art Deco period. This helped me make a decision about the style of my design and gave me the idea of simplifying the imagery into geometric shapes.
- When I was developing the lettering for my design, I experimented with different colour combinations and styles. I decided on a contrasting but harmonious colour combination of purple and turquoise. I also decided on an angular geometric style to contrast with the circles representing the fruit.
- I tried different ways of applying my idea to a variety of bottle shapes. I decided on a fairly conventional label shape as it would be more practical and cheap to produce.
- I feel that my solution will appeal to the target audience because the design is sophisticated and the purple, turquoise and black colour palette and geometric design will attract the older teenage target market rather than children.
- The bottle label is fit for purpose as it includes all of the important information stated in the design requirements, including a bar code and the volume.
- The design reflects the contents of the juice but in an original way. I feel that the repeating motif is eye-catching. The purple in the colour palette also reflects the juicy ingredients of berries.
- The multipack and the bottle label co-ordinate well as I have used circular motifs and the same colour scheme in both, but I reversed the colours in the lettering and imagery to make it more visually interesting.
- I think that the design will stand out on the supermarket shelves as it is different in style from other drinks on the market which tend to be bright colours with obvious illustrations of fruit. My design is more sophisticated, simple and elegant.
- If I was to redo the solution one modification which would improve the design would be to include nutritional information and recycling information.
- Another modification I would do if I had time would be to produce my design solution on the computer as I used pens to add colour and it is a little untidy when viewed close up. Working on the computer would give the design a more professional finish.

# 'Embroidery & embellishment'

## TEXTILE CASE STUDY

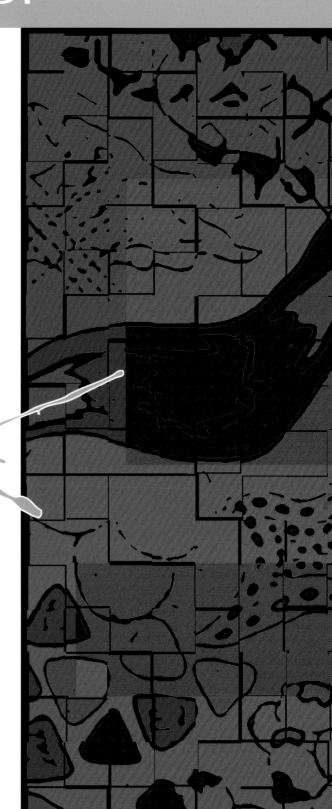

3

- Design brief
- Initial sampling
- Initial concept designs
- Corset development
- Design solution

# Design brief

| Fashion/Textiles Design Brief Worksheet | | | |
|---|---|---|---|
| **Name:** Amy | | **Class:** S4 | |

| Which of the following items do you intend to design? | | |
|---|---|---|
| Bag | Wrap | Fabric cuff |
| Cushion | Customised T-shirt | Fabric neckpiece |
| Skirt | (Corset) | Fabric corsage |
| The department will supply you with a basic pattern which you can adapt. | | |

| Identify your source of inspiration | |
|---|---|
| (Natural) | Manmade |
| Use this space to list some possibilities: | |
| *Snakes, geometric pattern, fashion, animal pattern and fabric manipulation.* | |
| **Final decision:** *To design and make a corset* | |

## Identify your target market

| Gender: | Age group: | | Personal style: | |
|---|---|---|---|---|
| Male | Teenage | 25+ | Stylish | Quirky |
| (Female) | 18–25 | 30+ | Funky | Classic |
| Unisex | (20–30) | Mature | Fashion conscious | Avant-garde |
| | 20+ | | Edgy | (Arty) |
| | | | Vintage | Punk |

## Designer influences

| Historical | | Contemporary | |
|---|---|---|---|
| Victoriana | | Zandra Rhodes | |
| Art Nouveau | | Vivienne Westwood | |
| (Art Deco) | *Erté* | (Alexander McQueen) | |
| Bauhaus | *Coco Chanel* | Jonathan Saunders | |
| 60s – Biba, Pierre Cardin | | Louise Gray | |
| 70s | | Holly Fulton | |
| 80s – Steven Sprouse | | Eiko Ishioka | |

## Materials and equipment required

| | | | |
|---|---|---|---|
| (Paper) | (Fabric) | (Sewing machine) | (Needles/Pins etc) |
| (Recycled material) | (Bondaweb) | (Felting machine) | Wet felting equipment |
| Plastic bags | Dissolvable Vilene | (Iron) | (Beads/Sequins) |
| (Thread) | (Embroidery threads) | T-shirt | Eyelets |

## Skills development required

| | | | |
|---|---|---|---|
| Pattern cutting | Making templates | (Hand sewing) | (Machine sewing) |
| (Beading) | Felt-making | (Appliqué) | Using heat gun |
| Hand dyeing | (Machine embroidery) | Making tassels/fringes | (Fabric manipulation) |
| Laminating/Lamifix | | | |

## Supported study workshops

Supported study is recommended – you will make more progress.
**NOTE:** If you have chosen to design a corset or a skirt, you **must** attend these workshops in order to make your basic garment.

Amy developed her design brief from a worksheet given to her by her class teacher. She took this information and created her own personalised design brief.

Inspired by Erté's work, Amy decided to focus on animal patterns, specifically snakeskin.

'I am going to design a corset for a special occasion. The client would like the garment to be eye-catching and unique. The corset is for a professional female who is 30 years old. The client likes Art Deco fashion but requires a modern twist. The client requires the garment to be embellished and embroidered. She likes decorative costume design.

The corset needs to be fitted and to have detailing that can be seen from a distance.'

# Initial sampling

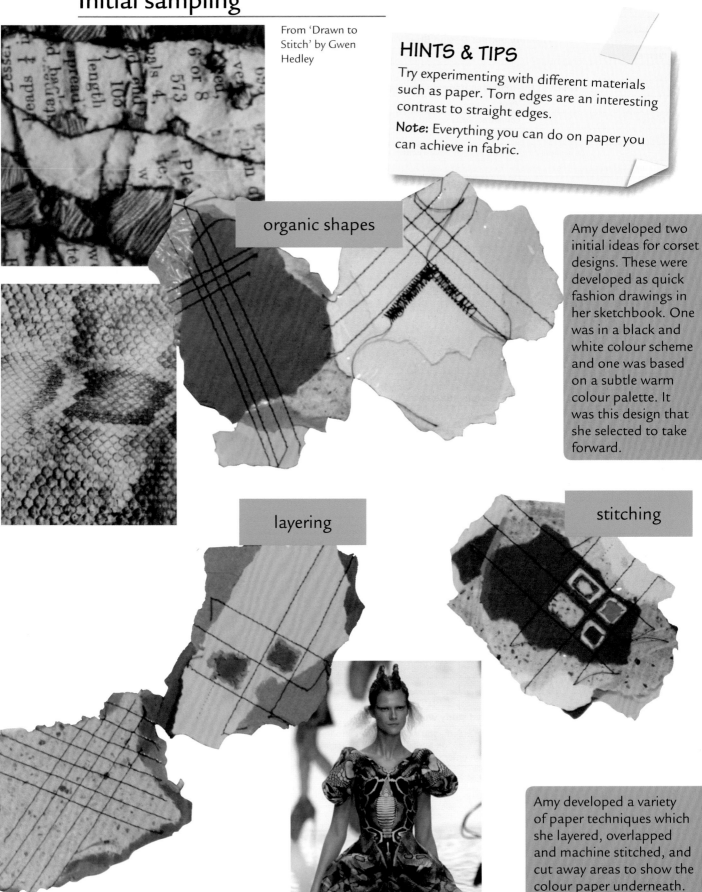

From 'Drawn to Stitch' by Gwen Hedley

organic shapes

Amy developed two initial ideas for corset designs. These were developed as quick fashion drawings in her sketchbook. One was in a black and white colour scheme and one was based on a subtle warm colour palette. It was this design that she selected to take forward.

layering

stitching

cutaways

Amy developed a variety of paper techniques which she layered, overlapped and machine stitched, and cut away areas to show the colour paper underneath. She wanted to try and develop some techniques that would have an emphasi on pattern.

Moth Dress (2010) by Alexander McQueen

# Design development

curvilinear

shape

snakeskin

Amy decided not to make all the circles perfectly circular but preferred the less precise organic look of her stitched paper samples.

Amy developed small- and large-scale circles which overlapped and draped around the body.

xpandaprint is an interesting technique to use to create raised circular surfaces

Corset by Stefanie Nieuwenhuyse

cutaway

Amy made drawings to explore the different shapes found in snakeskin. She then scanned a line drawing into the computer and added a limited colour palette based on one of her snakeskin images.

Amy studied Erté's work. She liked the Art Deco period in terms of finishes such as snakeskin and animal-inspired patterns. She liked the fact that Erté used embellishment in his fashion designs. Erté was known for his decorative style.

Costume design for Mme Ganna Wolska in 'Fidora', 1919 (gouache and gold and silver on paper), Erte, (Romain de Tirtoff) (1892–1990) / Private Collection

Amy wanted to develop her textile skills. She loved experimenting with texture and fabric and wanted to manipulate fabric through stitching, cutting and layering to achieve her final outcome.

# Technique development

Amy spent time experimenting with fabrics. She beaded samples made from different coloured fabrics. The beading added texture and highlighted the organic shapes that she previously developed.

Amy also worked on developing fabric samples. These were based on paper examples she had created in her sketchbook. Amy found that by using different weights of fabric the samples were more successful.

Amy particularly liked the use of the reversed denim in one of her layered samples. Her ideas began to focus on the development of embroidery over different combinations of woven textiles. She tried hand embroidery as well as machine stitching. Amy found it easier to annotate her sketches and samples as she was producing them. This meant she could remember the techniques used and why.

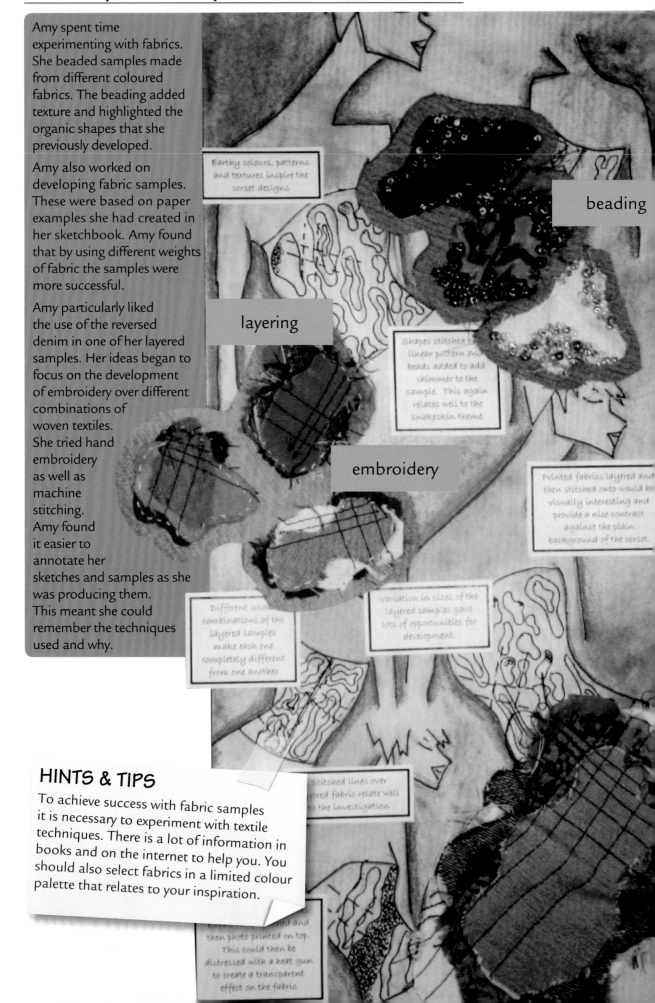

Earthy colours, patterns and textures inspire the corset designs

beading

layering

Shapes stitched by linear pattern and beads added to add shimmer to the sample. This again relates well to the snakeskin theme

embroidery

Printed fabrics layered and then stitched onto would be visually interesting and provide a nice contrast against the plain background of the corset.

Different colour combinations of the layered samples make each one completely different from one another

Variation in sizes of the layered samples gave lots of opportunities for development.

## HINTS & TIPS

To achieve success with fabric samples it is necessary to experiment with textile techniques. There is a lot of information in books and on the internet to help you. You should also select fabrics in a limited colour palette that relates to your inspiration.

Stitched lines over layered fabric relate well to the investigation

then photo printed on top. This could then be distressed with a heat gun to create a transparent effect on the fabric

# Design solution

Amy's art and design department specialised in fashion and textiles. The department offered supported study evenings on textile techniques and garment construction. Amy had no experience in dressmaking or sewing before she started this project. On the advice of her teacher she made a basic corset which was easy to construct and adapt. She concentrated on making textile embellishments which were related to her developments. Amy spent a lot of time hand sewing and beading at lunchtime and after school. She would have been unable to complete this garment without this extra time, which she committed herself to at the beginning of the project.

## COMMON MISTAKES

Sometimes students choose to do a fashion portfolio, but do not have the skills or the facilities to make the final outcome. While a drawing will communicate your idea to some extent, it is no substitute for a fully constructed concept garment. If you are working in fashion, it is good practice to create a 3D outcome. If you cannot do this, then a more realistic design brief might involve textile design, where you are designing the fabric only, or perhaps you could design a simpler textile item, such as a cushion or bag.

## NATIONAL 5 ART AND DESIGN – DESIGN PORTFOLIO EVALUATION

| Candidate name: | Amy | Candidate number: | 000000 |
| --- | --- | --- | --- |
| Centre number: | | 000000 | |

**Instructions to candidates**

You should reflect on and critically evaluate the creative process you followed when working through your design portfolio. In your evaluation give justified personal opinions on:

- the decisions you made when working through your portfolio
- the effectiveness of the aesthetic and functional qualities of your portfolio, referring to your design brief requirements.

**10 marks**

- I decided to focus on snakeskin as a source of inspiration and my investigation images helped me to develop my colour palette, which I deliberately restricted throughout the development.
- The market research and investigation into the Art Deco style which I carried out helped me to decide on the style of my corset which had to be Art Deco but with a modern twist. The animal print was very typical of Art Deco but I interpreted it using more contemporary fabric techniques and adding denim also helped bring it up to date.
- The work of Alexander McQueen inspired me to experiment with the silhouette of the corset and that is why I decided to include a shoulder piece.
- I feel my final design meets the design requirements demanded by the brief as the corset is very unique in terms of styling, shape and detailing. As it is a one-off, hand-made piece, this is not something that could be found on the high street.
- I feel that I used my source of inspiration in an unusual and creative way. I explored the organic shapes I saw in the snakeskin and developed these shapes into simplified patterns, which I experimented with using fabric techniques. These samples really helped me to decide on the embellishment techniques for the corset.
- I used appliqué techniques to develop the pattern as well as stitching and beadwork to add more pattern and texture which was very effective.
- I am pleased with the quality of construction and embellishment as I took a lot of care over making it. I had to learn how to make the basic corset on the sewing machine. I found using the machine difficult at first, but soon got used to it. Once I was confident with the machine, I also decided to use machine stitching in the decoration which contrasted well with the organic shapes.
- I believe the corset is suitable for special occasions as it is decorative and the decoration can be seen from a distance, which was a requirement of the brief. The beads and sequins catch the light and create some sparkle which adds to the visual impact.
- I believe that the corset would appeal to my client, a professional female aged 30. The design is sophisticated but also contemporary. It could be worn with jeans or dressed up more with a skirt.
- I am very pleased with my design. However, if I could change anything I would increase the amount of beading to add more texture to the corset. The added sparkle would make it more glamorous and even more suitable for evening occasions.

# DESIGN TECHNIQUES

**3**

- Motif development
- Architectural development
- Paper development
- 2D and 3D development

# Motif development

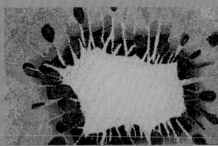

Some areas of design may require you to develop your own work. These may include jewellery, textiles and graphics. Design development is about making small changes and exhausting an idea. Having a limited colour palette allows you to concentrate on developing the motif through line, shape and pattern.

Sanna developed her kiwi fruit motif using design techniques such as simplifying, stylising, adding pattern, creating basic motifs and by developing repeat patterns.

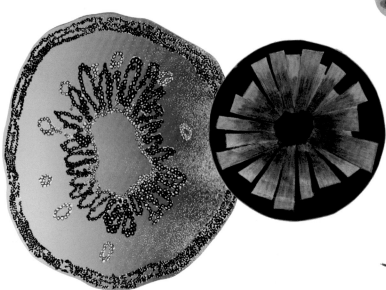

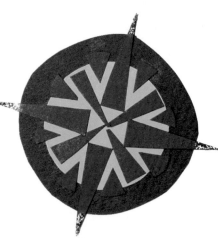

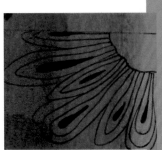

She tried using different media which included collage, print-making, coloured pencil and felt-tip pen. She kept a consistent and limited colour scheme which helped unify all her design concepts.

## HINTS & TIPS

Developing an idea is not always about major changes. Have fun and do not worry if there are ideas you do not like. Keep going and better ideas will happen. Design is all about development and experimentation.

# Architectural development

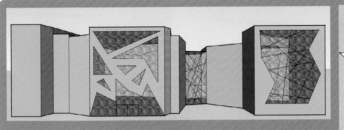

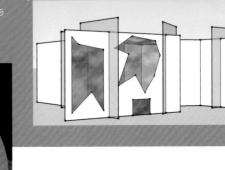

Architectural drawing can be achieved in a number of ways. These computer-aided drawings were created using the free software program Google Sketchup. It is simple and easy to use. By using this type of sketching method, you can see the building from a number of viewpoints and experiment with how it will look in different materials.

Sketch model-making is an excellent way to produce a mock-up of your idea. This type of model doesn't need to be highly finished. You can use paper and card and tape the pieces together. The main purpose is to help you to work out your ideas as part of your development.

You can draw your concept on a drawing board using single-point or two-point perspective to create a realistic image of your design.

# Paper development

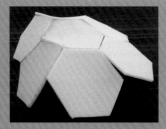

Paper mock-ups are a great method of visualising your ideas 3-dimensionally. You begin by using white paper and create your concepts by folding, cutting, layering and manipulating your paper into a design. You will find that creating your 3D idea in this way will help solve problems such as fit, function and construction.

Remember, if you cannot make your idea in paper or card, you may struggle in any other material. During this process your ideas will change – this is called development.

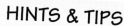

## HINTS & TIPS

You could use acrylic paint, spray paint or tissue paper to achieve a good-quality finish.

By completing paper developments in the early stages of the design process, you can then experiment with a variety of finishes to create the aesthetic appeal that suits your design brief. Paper can be treated in different ways to give convincing finishes which can be used to produce final outcomes. It can be made to look like metal, plastic or leather, for example.

# 2D to 3D development

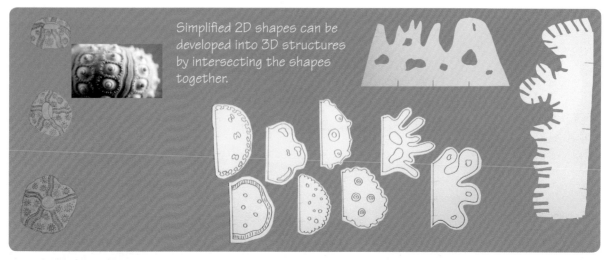

Simplified 2D shapes can be developed into 3D structures by intersecting the shapes together.

Developing 2D shapes into 3D form can be really simple. Try cutting out multiples of the same 2D shape and then cut slots in the shapes. Slot the pieces together to create a variety of 3D forms.

Paper mock-ups help solve a number of design problems, from function to style.

3D paper forms can then be developed into designs using a number of other materials.

Chapter 4

# 4     The Question Paper

The question paper is worth 20% of the overall mark. Your score can make the difference between a pass and a fail, or between one grade and another, so it is well worth putting in the effort to prepare for the question paper to maximise your mark. If you find this kind of work challenging, there are skills and techniques you can learn to help you. The time allocation for the paper is **1 hour 30 minutes**.

## Structure of the question paper

| Section 1 Art studies | • **Q1** – You **must** answer this question. Part (a) should be based on **two artworks** that you have studied. In part (b) you should select **one artist** from part (a) and describe how two different influences can be seen in any of their work.<br>• **Q2–Q6** – Choose **one** question from the selection. Select the question you feel most confident about answering. |
|---|---|
| Section 2 Design studies | • **Q7** – You **must** answer this question. Part (a) should based on **two designs** that you have studied. In part (b) select **one designer** from part (a) and describe how two different influences can be seen in any of their work.<br>• **Q8–Q12** – Choose **one** question from the selection. You should select the design category you are most familiar with. |

## Mark breakdown of the question paper

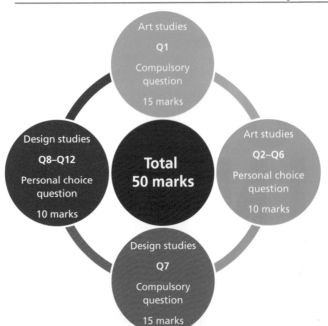

Art studies
Q1
Compulsory question
15 marks

Art studies
Q2–Q6
Personal choice question
10 marks

Total
50 marks

Design studies
Q8–Q12
Personal choice question
10 marks

Design studies
Q7
Compulsory question
15 marks

### National 4

You are not required to sit a question paper.

You will be assessed on your critical studies within your expressive and design units.

The information in this section will be helpful to you when you are studying the work of artists and designers in your units.

# Time management in the exam

You have **1 hour 30 minutes** in which to complete the question paper. This means that you have a few minutes to read the paper and decide on your personal choice questions. You should then spend around 25 minutes on each response to the compulsory questions Q1 and Q7, and 15–20 minutes on each of your two optional questions.

# Exam technique

In art and design studies, many issues affect each other. For instance, when discussing materials, you can comment on how the choice of materials affects the style of a design. When explaining an artist's technique, you could discuss how colour is applied, and so on. The example questions and answers in this chapter should help you to develop your exam technique and learn how to respond effectively to the questions asked.

# Preparing for the question paper

There are a number of techniques that will help you to prepare for the exam:

Try making up your own questions and marking schemes. This is a great way to understand the format of the paper and the terminology used in questions. Get a friend to do the same. You can swap questions to test each other.

Revise the meanings of art and design terms. You could create visual flashcards. Think about how you might illustrate the words *tone* or *perspective*, for instance.

**Practise!**

Work by yourself or with a friend to map out or list possible responses to questions. Challenge yourself to write down as many relevant points as you can within a time limit.

Start with some basic descriptive statements and add explanations and justifications. For example, how would you extend the point '*this painting has been created using bright colours*'?

## COMMON MISTAKES

A lot of candidates think that reading through notes is an effective way to study. For most students, this approach does not work and is a very poor way to prepare for an exam. It is important that you try to learn in an 'active' way. This means using methods like those suggested above and practising as much as you can.

## HINTS & TIPS

Start each answer on a new page. This means that if you have time at the end of the exam, you can revisit earlier questions and add to them. Don't forget to number your answers to indicate which personal choice questions you have attempted.

# Section 1: Expressive art studies

## Question 1: Expressive art studies compulsory question

These questions test your knowledge and understanding of the artworks you have studied during the course.

In this question, you will:

- Select **two artworks** by different artists who have worked on the same subject matter and/or theme.

- Compare how **three** elements (specified in the question) have been used to create these artworks.

- Give an opinion on an aspect specified in the question with **two** justified reasons.

- Select **one artist** whose artwork you have discussed in part (a). Identify two influences on this artist and describe how these influences can be seen in any of their work.

## HINTS & TIPS
You cannot predict what will come up in the exam as the content of the questions will change from year to year. Therefore, it is recommended that you have a knowledge of several works of art so that you are able to respond to any question.

Expressive art issues you may be asked about in this question include:

| | |
|---|---|
| **Composition or arrangement** | arrangement; pose (in figure and portrait work); setting; viewpoint; focal point; choice of subject matter; perspective; proportion; scale and use of space |
| **Subject matter or imagery** | choice of subject matter; sources of inspiration and influences; effect on the work |
| **Visual elements** | line; tone; colour; shape; form; texture; pattern; how they have been combined/applied; their effect on the work |
| **Media handling and techniques** | choice of media and processes; application of media; effect on style; treatment of subject matter; level of detail; expressive qualities; skills demonstrated; 2D or 3D; scale of the work; influences on technique |
| **Style** | aims and influence of specific art movements; what makes the work distinctive; sources of inspiration; the artists' 'trademarks'; artists' response to the subject |
| **Scale** | the dimensions of the work; large or small; effect of scale on the work; effect of scale on detail/realism/visual impact, etc. |
| **Mood and atmosphere** | the mood and atmosphere created and how this has been achieved (e.g. colour, use of media, subject matter, composition, style, etc.); what the work communicates to you and why |
| **Influences** | influences on the artist's work and practice, such as local or world events, politics, religion, personal circumstances, health, relationships, other artists and art movements, nature, literature, philosophy, science and technology |

## Question 1 examples

### Example A

Identify **two artworks** by different artists that you have studied. These should be based on similar subject matter and/or the same theme.

(a) With reference to these two selected artworks, comment on:

- composition or arrangement
- colour
- style.

Which of the two works do you find most appealing? Give **two** justified reasons.

**Total marks    10**

(b) Select **one artist** from part (a).

Identify **two** influences on this artist **and** describe how these influences can be seen in any of their work.

**Total marks    5**

### Example B

Identify **two artworks** by different artists that you have studied. These should be based on similar subject matter and/or the same theme.

(a) With reference to these two selected artworks, comment on:

- media handling and/or technique
- scale
- mood and atmosphere.

Which of the two works is most effective at communicating the subject or theme? Give **two** justified reasons.

**Total marks    10**

(b) Select **one artist** from part (a).

Identify **two** influences on this artist **and** describe how these influences can be seen in any of their work.

**Total marks    5**

### Example C

Identify **two artworks** by different artists that you have studied. These should be based on similar subject matter and/or the same theme.

(a) With reference to these two selected artworks, comment on:

- composition or arrangement
- line
- mood and atmosphere.

Which of the two works is your personal favourite? Give **two** justified reasons.

**Total marks    10**

(b) Select **one** artist from part (a).

Identify **two** influences on this artist **and** describe how these influences can be seen in any of their work.

**Total marks    5**

### Example D

Identify **two artworks** by different artists that you have studied. These should be based on similar subject matter and/or the same theme.

(a) With reference to these two selected artworks, comment on:

- subject matter and/or imagery
- media handling and/or technique
- pattern.

Which of the two works is the most interesting? Give **two** justified reasons.

**Total marks    10**

(b) Select **one artist** from part (a).

Identify **two** influences on this artist **and** describe how these influences can be seen in any of their work.

**Total marks    5**

## Question 1 example answers

## Response to example A

| Emily's first attempt – a basic response | Teacher's notes |
|---|---|
| (a) Two works by different artists I have studied are 'Le Vase Paille' by Paul Cézanne, painted in 1895, and 'Still Life Looking towards Stromboli and Panarea' by Leon Morrocco, which is a contemporary painting. | Explain what they have in common – theme? subject? |
| Cézanne's painting consists of a group of objects and fruit on a table top. There is also a vase and a tablecloth. Morrocco's painting also shows fruit on a tabletop but is set on a beach. There are two plates of fruit and what looks like a patterned cloth. There is also a small figure to the side of the table. | This is very descriptive. Use the key words in the question in your response and show your knowledge of art terms that we have covered in class. Refer to the wordbanks. |
| The paintings are different styles but both artists use distortion. | In what way? |
| The colour in Cézanne's painting is dull as there is a lot of brown. Morrocco's painting is much brighter. There is a lot of blue because of the sea behind the table. | Use your knowledge of colour theory to explain more effectively how colour is used. |
| The work I find the most appealing is the Leon Morrocco still life. This is because it has bright colours and includes the sea. | You have given two reasons but you will not be given marks for points you have already made.

We will do some more work in class to prepare for this question. Some paired work will help you tackle these questions more effectively.

Consider using sub-headings to ensure that you answer all aspects of the question in depth. |
| (b) Cézanne was born in Aix-en-Provence in 1839. | Is this an influence on his work? You need to be more specific.
How did where he was born influence his work? |
| His father wanted him to be a lawyer but Cézanne wanted to be an artist. | Is this relevant? Can you find out anything about how it influenced the way he worked? If not leave it out. |
| He met the Impressionist artists and worked with Pissarro for a while but he did not like working in the Impressionist style so he went on to be a Post-Impressionist. | There is quite a lot to explore here. Give more detail and some examples of paintings. You could explain more about the Impressionist and Post-Impressionist styles. |
| Cézanne's father died in 1886 and left him a lot of money. | You need to explain how this affected his work. |
| Cézanne sadly died in 1906 aged 67. | Leave this fact out as it is not relevant to the question asked. Remember that you only need to write about two influences in detail. |

### HINTS & TIPS
You only need to name two influences on the artist. However, to get full marks, you need to write about three different ways these can be seen in the work. So you should give one example for one influence and two examples for the other.

| Emily's next attempt – a more in-depth and effective response | Marks |
|---|---|
| (a) Two works by different artists I have studied are 'Le Vase Paille' by Paul Cézanne, painted in 1895, and 'Still Life Looking towards Stromboli and Panarea' by Leon Morrocco, which is a contemporary painting. They are both still life paintings of fruit and objects arranged on table tops. | |

Composition

Cézanne's painting has a triangular composition with a vase at the apex of the triangle. The sides of the triangle are suggested by the perspective of the tabletop. For me, this makes the vase the focal point of the painting. The background is plain, with textural brushstrokes which do not distract too much from the objects. The perspective is unusual with the tabletop tilted towards the viewer and items placed off the horizontal and vertical. Cézanne was known for altering perspective. Morrocco's painting also experiments with perspective, which is flattened even more than in Cézanne's. The table is set against a background of sky and sea. There is also a small figure to the side of the table and a boat which, along with the horizon line, helps give the painting distance and depth. I would say there is no one focal point to this busy painting, as my eye tends to wander around the composition from object to object.

Colour

Cézanne's colour palette is mainly warm tertiary colours, but these are balanced in places with jewel-like greens, yellows and oranges. The drab background helps keep my attention on the fruit.

Morrocco's painting is much brighter with saturated colours. The painting is dominated by the cold blue background but is balanced by the warm pink tabletop and the hot colours of the fruit.

Style

The paintings are different styles but both artists use distortion. Cézanne's distorted perspective was a key part of his Post-Impressionist style, as he was not concerned with painting reality but with creating balance and harmony in his work.

The artists both use oil paint but applied in a different way. Cézanne uses directional brushstrokes and broken outlines. Paint is applied in thin transparent layers to build up the colour. Cézanne would sometimes take months or even years to finish a painting as he was a perfectionist constantly striving for harmony.

Morrocco's painting has flatter, more opaque colour, but has textural areas here and there. He uses bolder outlines than Cézanne.

The painting I find most appealing is the Morrocco still life. I love its vibrant colour which reminds me of hot sunny days. The artist has really captured the feeling of the hot weather with the deep cobalt blue sky. The subject matter and the background of blue sky and sea give me happy memories of being on holiday. The background makes it clear to the viewer that it is a scene from a hot country.

## HINTS & TIPS

Some candidates prefer to use sub-headings to structure their answers. You do not have to do this. Use whatever technique works for you, as long as you respond to the question asked effectively.

| | |
|---|---|
| (b) Cézanne met the Impressionist artists and worked with Pissarro for a while, which influenced his work. He learned how to paint in an Impressionist style. An example of work from this period is 'The House of the Hanged Man'. In this painting, the broken brushstrokes and dappled colour typical of the Impressionists can be seen. | ✓ ✓ |
| However, Cézanne did not like working in the Impressionist style and he went on to develop his own style. He preferred to work slowly and to revisit his paintings over a long period of time. Examples of his Post-Impressionist works include many still lifes of objects in his studio. He often painted the same objects over and over again trying to achieve perfection. | ✓ |
| Cézanne's father died in 1886 and left him a lot of money, which influenced his art career. He was not successful at selling work in his own lifetime. This inheritance meant he could carry on working as an artist and keep working in his own individual Post-Impressionist style which was thought to be very radical at the time. | ✓ ✓ |
| You have made more than 10 valid justified points in part (a) and you have answered part (b) effectively. You only need to write 10 points for part (a) so think about how you could streamline your responses for the final exam. Good use of art terminology. The group work tasks in class have really helped your exam technique. Well done! | 15 |

## Response to example C

| Beth's response | Marks |
|---|---|
| (a) Two works by different artists I have studied are 'Weeping Woman' by Pablo Picasso, painted in 1937, and 'The Troubled City' by Ken Currie, painted in 1991. Both paintings are responses to the theme of conflict. | |

### Composition

Picasso's painting is a portrait, concentrating on a head and shoulders. It is not always clear with Picasso which way the subject is facing as he uses multiple viewpoints. This can be seen in this painting as the subject appears to be facing us, but is in side profile at the same time. The woman appears to be in a room, which is suggested by the shapes in the background. The focal point of this painting is the subject's eyes, which remind me of broken and shattered windows.  ✓ ✓

Ken Currie's painting is a figure composition and is very complex. It is a large crowd scene with a tangle of figures receding all the way to the background, which appears to be burning buildings. The ladder being carried creates a vertical line which leads your eye to the figure with the megaphone, which for me is the focal point.  ✓ ✓

### Line

Lines are used to outline and emphasise the jagged geometric shapes in Picasso's painting. The hair is also simplified and depicted with bold lines. This is typical of Picasso's Cubist style, where objects are represented through line and shape. This technique flattens the perspective.  ✓ ✓

In Currie's painting, outlines are often blurred and indistinct, which gives the impression of figures dissolving into the shadows. This helps to add to the confusion of the scene.  ✓

### Mood and atmosphere

Both paintings have very different styles but, as both depict conflict, they both convey a disturbing atmosphere. Picasso's painting was about the Spanish Civil War and this suggests that the woman is mourning or grieving for someone lost, or perhaps about what is happening to Spain. This is shown by the fact that she is holding a handkerchief to her face and by the expressive colour and shapes used.  ✓

I am not sure what the conflict is about in Currie's painting, but it also suggests civil war with rioting and looting. The skull-like faces of the figures and their decaying flesh suggests death and portrays a dark, sinister atmosphere. The burning city and weapons being carried by many of the figures suggest destruction and violence.  ✓ ✓

I like both paintings but my personal favourite is by Ken Currie. Although it is distressing to look at, it shows conflict in a very graphic way. This is achieved through the horrifying subject matter. It is full of people who are either attacking violently or who are wounded. Wounds are shown like slash marks on their bodies. His style of painting with its sombre colours and deep, dark tones helps to convey the horrors of war very effectively.  ✓ ✓

| | |
|---|---|
| (b) The Spanish Civil War was an influence on Picasso. He produced a number of paintings in reaction to this. 'Weeping Woman' is one of these with its fractured composition and jagged edges showing Picasso's emotions about the war. | ✓<br>✓ |
| Another painting from this time is Guernica, which is a complicated figure composition showing the bombing of the town of Guernica. The painting is large scale, striking and monochromatic and contains many symbols to do with the war. | ✓ |
| Picasso's relationship with Dora Maar is also an influence on 'Weeping Woman'. She was an artist and photographer and she encouraged Picasso's work during this period. Their stormy relationship affected his Cubist style at this time, which became more harsh and geometric. | ✓<br>✓ |
| More than 10 justified points have been made in response to part (a) and you have answered part (b) well. It is clear that you understand the key points about the paintings. An excellent personal response! | 15 |

## Questions 2–6: Expressive art studies personal choice question

You will choose **one question** to answer from this selection. This part of the question paper is all about responding to an unseen image. You will be applying what you have learned in your critical studies. The marker will expect to see you demonstrate knowledge and understanding of art practice and to be able to apply terminology correctly.

Each question has a related image. These will change from year to year, but you can get an idea of the variety likely to come up by looking at SQA's specimen question paper and past papers. You can also prepare for this part of the paper by trying to broaden your experience of art in general.

Once you have read through this section, along with the worked examples, have a go at answering the questions. There are no 'right answers', but your responses should show a knowledge and understanding of critical studies.

You can expect to find a variety of genres and approaches in the paper, such as:

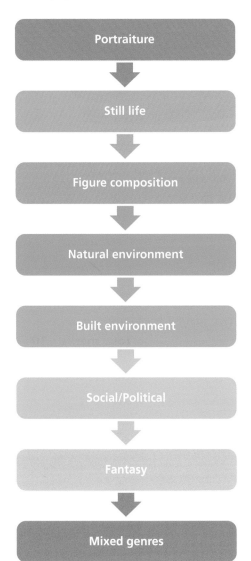

- Portraiture
- Still life
- Figure composition
- Natural environment
- Built environment
- Social/Political
- Fantasy
- Mixed genres

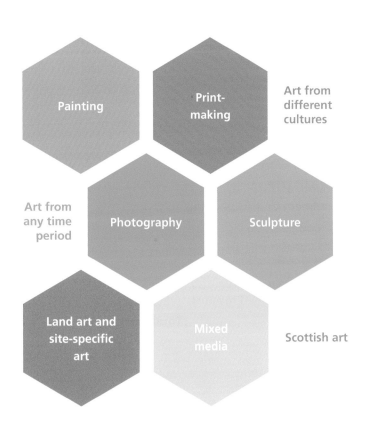

- Painting
- Print-making
- Art from different cultures
- Art from any time period
- Photography
- Sculpture
- Land art and site-specific art
- Mixed media
- Scottish art

## Questions 2–6 examples

### Art from other cultures and times

In the question paper, examples of artwork from ancient times to the present day may be represented. You may also find artworks from other cultures. You will probably be familiar with Western art, but it is a good idea to look at some artworks from other cultures. This will increase your confidence in discussing less familiar artworks and will extend your choice in the exam.

*Emperor Jahangir Receiving his Two Sons* (1605–06) by Manohar
Gouache on paper (20.8 cm × 15.4 cm)

*The Goddess Tara* (1426–35) by an unknown artist
Bronze, gold, gilding and paint
(26.6 cm × 16.3 cm × 15 cm)

## Example A

Comment on this painting, referring to:

- composition
- colour
- pattern.

What is your opinion of this style of painting? Give **two** justified reasons.

**Total marks 10**

## Example B

Comment on this sculpture, referring to:

- pose
- decoration
- materials.

What does this sculpture communicate to you? Give **two** justified reasons.

**Total marks 10**

## Response to example B

| Robyn's first, descriptive response | Robyn's second, more analytical response |
|---|---|
| <u>Pose</u><br><br>The goddess is sitting cross-legged with one hand raised. She is looking downwards. | <u>Pose</u><br><br>The goddess is sitting cross-legged with one hand raised. This reminds me of a yoga position and makes her look like she is meditating. She is looking downwards which adds to the idea that she may be meditating or thinking. Her face reminds me of a Buddha. |
| <u>Decoration</u><br><br>There is a lot of decoration on the statue. It is sitting on a decorative base. She is wearing a crown and jewellery. There are flowers growing up and intertwining with her arms. | <u>Decoration</u><br><br>There is a lot of decoration on the statue. The goddess is covered in jewellery. There is decorative jewellery around her neck and waist, and bracelets on her wrists. She is wearing large, heavy earrings. This makes her look rich and opulent. She is wearing a very ornate crown which makes her seem important. The style of the clothing and jewellery looks Eastern or oriental. There are flowers growing up and intertwining with her arms. This makes her look like she is connected with nature in some way.<br><br>The statue is sitting on a very decorative base. It reminds me of a scallop shell and reinforces the idea that the goddess is something to do with nature. |
| <u>Materials</u><br><br>The statue is made of bronze and gold with gilding and paint. | <u>Materials</u><br><br>The statue is made of bronze, and although it is a small statue it will be quite heavy. The shiny, gold finish reminds me of royalty as I associate this colour with wealth and status. The attention to detail in this small sculpture is amazing and it must have been made by a very skilled artist. |
| <u>What it communicates to me</u><br><br>The statue does not look like a typical goddess.<br><br>Try to develop these by thinking about the effect achieved and the reasons why the artist has made the sculpture like this. | <u>What it communicates to me</u><br><br>The statue does not look like a typical goddess as I am used to the idea of classical Greek or Roman goddesses and this depiction of a goddess looks very exotic and oriental. The Goddess Tara, with her peaceful expression, looks as if she is a kind and caring goddess.<br><br>Excellent response! |

## HINTS & TIPS

Generally, you will be awarded one mark for each well-justified point made which is relevant to the question being asked. Remember that you will need to respond to all aspects of the question to gain full marks.

## Sculpture and site-specific art

*Family Group* (1948–49) by Henry Moore
Bronze (154 cm × 118 cm × 70 cm)

### Example C

Comment on this sculpture, referring to:

- arrangement
- form
- style.

What mood does this work suggest to you?
Give **two** justified reasons.

**Total marks    10**

*Touchstone North* (1990) by Andy Goldsworthy
Stone

### Example D

Comment on this artwork, referring to:

- arrangement
- shape and/or form
- materials.

What is your opinion of this approach to
sculpture? Give **two** justified reasons.

**Total marks    10**

*Flying Pins* (2000) by Claes van Oldenburg
and Coosje van Bruggen
Steel, fibre-reinforced plastic, PVC foam, painted
with polyester gelcoat and polyurethane enamel
(Each pin is 7.5 m high)

### Example E

Comment on this sculpture, referring to:

- scale
- arrangement
- subject matter.

What is your personal response to this
sculpture? Give **two** justified reasons.

**Total marks    10**

# Drawing, painting and printmaking

*La Jupe Verte* (*The Green Skirt*) (c.1897–1901)
by Edgar Degas
Pastel on paper (45 cm × 37 cm)

## Example F

Comment on this artwork, referring to:

- composition
- line
- colour.

How successful is this technique? Give **two** justified reasons.

**Total marks    10**

*Sandwich and Soda* (1964) by Roy Lichtenstein
Screenprint on acetate (48.5 cm × 58.4 cm)

## Example G

Comment on this print, referring to:

- composition
- colour
- shape.

What is your opinion of this style of work? Give **two** justified reasons.

**Total marks    10**

*Head of a Woman* (15th century)
by Andrea del Verrocchio
Chalk on paper (32.5 cm × 27.2 cm)

## Example H

Comment on this drawing, referring to:

- composition
- line
- tone.

What does this work communicate to you? Give **two** justified reasons.

**Total marks    10**

Response to example H

| Sanna's response | Marks |
|---|---|
| <u>Composition</u><br><br>'Head of a Woman' by Andrea del Verrocchio is a portrait study. The composition is unusual in that it is closed in, concentrating only on the head. The subject is gazing downwards. In most portraits I have seen, the subject is looking at the viewer. This makes the subject appear shy. Her head is tilted to one side and the viewpoint is a three-quarter profile rather than facing straight on. This also adds to the idea that she is turning away from the artist and is self-conscious. | ✓<br>✓<br><br>✓ |
| <u>Line</u><br><br>Line has been used very sensitively and the artist must have had a very high level of skill to be able to draw like this. Line is used to define the features, but it is soft and not heavy and used in a delicate way. There is great attention to detail, with every line in the hair carefully drawn. The artist seems to have been particularly interested in the girl's hair style, which appears to be drawn more precisely than the rest of the study. Every detail of the plaits has been picked out in line. | ✓<br>✓<br>✓<br>✓ |
| <u>Tone</u><br><br>Tone has been used to suggest form and to model the features of the girl's face. Shadows and highlights have been depicted and the tone is softly blended. A wide tonal range has been used, from very dark to very light, and this helps to give the drawing a sense of realism. | ✓<br>✓ |
| What this drawing communicates to me is that it was probably a study for a painting. Many artists make drawings before they attempt a finished piece and I think that is what has happened here. I think the girl was probably posing for the artist in this way, so that she could be included in a larger painting later. The girl in the portrait looks mysterious because she is looking downwards and we cannot see her eyes. It makes me wonder what she is thinking about. | ✓<br><br>✓ |
| This is an excellent response and more than 10 points have been made. I like how you have demonstrated your knowledge of artists' methods in the conclusions, rather than just repeating points already made. | 10 |

## HINTS & TIPS

Sanna has been clever in this response by including some relevant facts about how artists work. If you find you are running out of steam in a response, think about all the general facts you have learned and see if there are any that can be applied to the question.

## COMMON MISTAKES

Many candidates leave the exam room and discuss the exam with their teacher or friends. Quite often, they say 'I was going to write that but I thought it was wrong!' There are no right or wrong answers in this subject, only justified observations and opinions. If you write something irrelevant, the marker will ignore it. You may not gain marks, but marks will not be deducted either, so you have nothing to lose.

*Window in Menton* (1948) by Anne Redpath
Oil on plywood (109.2 cm × 83.8 cm)

## Example I

Comment on this painting, referring to:

- composition
- colour
- pattern.

What mood and atmosphere does this painting communicate to you? Give **two** justified reasons.

**Total marks   10**

*The Aviary, Clifton* (1888) by Joseph Crawhall
Watercolour on paper (51 cm × 35 cm)

## Example J

Comment on this painting, referring to:

- composition
- colour
- media handling.

How well has the artist captured the subject matter? Give **two** justified reasons.

**Total marks   10**

*Autumn in Glencairn, Moniaive* (1887) by James Paterson
Oil on canvas (102 cm × 127 cm)

## Example K

Comment on this painting, referring to:

- composition
- colour
- technique.

What mood and atmosphere does this painting communicate? Give **two** justified reasons.

**Total marks   10**

*Still Life before an Open Window, Place Ravignan* (1915) by Juan Gris
Oil on canvas (115.9 cm × 88.9 cm)

## Example M

Comment on this painting, referring to:

■ composition
■ shape
■ colour.

What is your opinion of this style of painting? Give **two** justified reasons.

**Total marks    10**

*The Four Horsemen of the Apocalypse* (1498) by Albrecht Dürer
Woodcut print on paper (39.4 cm × 28.1 cm)

## Example L

Comment on this print, referring to:

■ composition
■ line
■ imagery.

What mood and atmosphere does this work communicate to you? Give **two** justified reasons.

**Total marks    10**

## Mixed media

*Dr Tom Normand* (1998) by Steven Campbell
Mixed media on canvas (182 cm × 97 cm)

### Example N

Comment on this artwork, referring to:

- composition
- colour
- technique.

What does the artist communicate about the subject of this work? Give **two** justified reasons.

**Total marks    10**

*Children and Chalked Wall 3* (1962) by Joan Eardley
Oil, newspaper and metal foil on canvas
(61 cm × 68.6 cm)

### Example O

Comment on this painting, referring to:

- pose
- texture
- colour.

What does the artist communicate about the character of the children? Give **two** justified reasons.

**Total marks    10**

### COMMON MISTAKES

Sometimes candidates do not read the question properly. If important aspects have been missed you cannot gain full marks.

### HINTS & TIPS

When choosing your personal expressive art studies question, don't automatically go for the image you consider 'easiest'. You may have more to say about the images you consider to be more challenging. You have a few minutes at the start of the exam to weigh this up and make a decision.

## Response to example N

| Beth's first descriptive response | Beth's second more analytical response |
|---|---|
| <u>Composition</u><br><br>The subject is sitting on a tall stool. He is in a room. There is lettering spelling his name on the right-hand side. The subject is looking out of the picture. | <u>Composition</u><br><br>The subject is sitting on a tall stool looking directly at the viewer. His pose is relaxed, with his legs crossed and his arms also crossed over on his knees. The setting appears to be a room. There seems to be a wall behind the subject with some pictures.<br><br>The viewpoint is eye level with the subject. This is a large-scale piece suggesting the subject is life size.<br><br>The perspective is quite flat but there is a sense that the stool is sitting on the floor. This is suggested by an area of lighter tone.<br><br>One unusual thing about the composition is the lettering spelling his name on the right-hand side. It is arranged vertically, which mirrors the vertical line made by the subject on the other side. There is also a 'shadow' behind the subject, which is like a mirror image of the subject in silhouette. |
| <u>Colour</u><br><br>The colours are dull. He has used browns and a dark red. | <u>Colour</u><br><br>The colours are drab browns and creams with accents of a dark red. These are warm tones. The effect is of warm, neutral colours. |
| <u>Technique</u><br><br>The artist has used mixed media. It looks as if he has used collage. There are drips of paint.<br><br>I have not seen a portrait like this before. It is very unusual.<br><br>Remember to use the art terms you learned about in class. You have also been taught how to analyse a composition, so look at your notes. You should also refer to your critical studies wordbanks to help you write a more detailed response. | <u>Technique</u><br><br>The artist has used mixed media. It looks as if he has used collage. There is what appears to be a sketchbook on the floor and pictures on the walls. It looks as if these are pictures and printed papers which the artist has stuck on. Watery drips of paint have run down the canvas creating an interesting textural effect. The lettering is very flat and has a 1960s style. It also looks as if it has been cut out and stuck on. A 'halo' of white paint has been applied around the subject, which adds emphasis.<br><br>The figure is painted quite realistically, but the face is slightly stylised as the eyes have been made larger than normal. This focuses your attention on his face.<br><br><u>What the artist communicates</u><br><br>I have not seen a portrait like this before. It is very unusual that the subject's name has been included, especially so large. This suggests that he is an important person. When I saw the title, I thought he looked very young to be a doctor, but the painting suggests that he is a person at ease with himself. This is because of the subject's relaxed body language and the fact he is looking directly at the viewer.<br><br>Much better response! |

# Photography

*Migrant Mother* (c.1936) by Dorothea Lange
Gelatin-silver print (38 cm × 49 cm)

## Example P

Comment on this photograph, referring to:

- composition
- subject matter
- lighting.

What mood and atmosphere is conveyed by the image? Give **two** justified reasons.

**Total marks    10**

*Big Cycling Race, Madison Square Garden, New York* (1932) by Fred Zinnemann
Gelatin-silver print (16.8 cm × 11.5 cm)

## Example Q

Comment on this photograph, referring to:

- camera angle
- shape
- tone.

How well has the photographer captured the mood of the event? Give **two** justified reasons.

**Total marks    10**

Photograph from *The Last Resort* series (1983–85) by Martin Parr

## Example R

Comment on this photograph, referring to:

- subject matter
- composition
- mood and atmosphere.

What is your opinion of this style of photography? Give **two** justified reasons.

**Total marks    10**

## Response to example Q

| Jacob's response | Marks |
|---|---|
| 'Big Cycling Race, Madison Square Garden, New York' by Fred Zinnemann makes use of a camera angle with a viewpoint above the subjects. This allows the photographer to look down on the race and to capture the cyclists going past at just the right moment. His angle of view means that the spectators are also in the frame. This helps to create a sense of distance, with the closer spectators in the foreground and the smaller spectators in the background giving a sense of perspective to the scene. | ✓<br><br>✓ |
| There is a dominant curved shape created by the track, which seems to be in a velodrome as it is at a steep angle. This leads your eye into the picture and to the cyclists coming around the bend, which is the focal point of the picture. The silhouettes of the spectators who are wearing hats give an idea that this is a historical photograph without you even having to look at the date. The cyclists have an indistinct shape as they are moving. This gives a sense of speed. | ✓<br>✓<br><br>✓ |
| There is a range of tones, but the image is mainly dark as the crowd is in shadow. Only the race track is illuminated, which is another reason it is the focal point of the image. The image is high contrast, with a few midtones. | ✓<br>✓<br>✓ |
| I think this image captures an atmosphere of excitement. This is suggested by members of the crowd all standing up and leaning forward. This mood of excitement is also communicated by the moment the picture was taken from that particular angle. It looks as if four cyclists are in the lead and it is uncertain who is going to win, which adds to the suspense of the crowd. | ✓ |
| The speed of the cyclists conveyed by the motion blur also adds to the excitement of the scene. | ✓ |
| Your answer shows a good understanding of issues relating to photography. You have written a lot of valid and well reasoned points, scoring full marks. | 10 |

### HINTS & TIPS

Remember that photography has its own terminology. It is said that photography is like 'painting with light'. You can discuss the effect of light and shade, camera angles and camera techniques on the image. Think about how the subject has been framed and whether it was 'set up' or something the photographer saw and responded to.

### COMMON MISTAKES

Sometimes candidates do not read the information given about the work and respond to a photograph or a sculpture as if it were a painting, discussing paint techniques, for instance. Be careful to read the caption under the work so that you do not make this mistake.

# Section 2: Design studies

## Question 7: Design studies compulsory question

This question tests your knowledge and understanding of designers' work and design issues you have studied during the course.

In this question, you will:

- Select **two designs** by different designers who have worked in the same area of design.

- Compare how **three** design issues (specified in the question) have been considered while creating these designs.

- Give an opinion on an aspect specified in the question with **two** justified reasons.

- Select **one designer** whose design you have discussed in part (a). Identify **two** influences on this designer **and** describe how these influences can be seen in any of their work.

### HINTS & TIPS

It is important that you have a knowledge of works by at least two designers. These designers must work in the same design area, for example, two graphic designers, two product designers, two jewellery designers, etc.

Try to find designers who have contrasting styles and approaches.

Design issues you may be asked about in the question include:

| | |
|---|---|
| **Function/Fitness for purpose** | purpose; primary and secondary functions; effectiveness; durability; practicality/wearability; safety; ergonomics/user-friendliness |
| **Aesthetics/Style** | visual impact; visual elements (line, tone, colour, shape, form, texture, pattern); how visual elements have been used/combined; influences of other designers/design movements; sources of inspiration; scale; detail; decoration |
| **Materials and techniques** | choice of materials; processes used; use of technology; production/construction methods; skills demonstrated; effect on the function and appearance of the design; suitability; cost |
| **Target market/Audience** | the market/audience the design is aimed at; consumer type; client; age group; gender; income bracket; interests; preferences; personality type |
| **Influences** | influences on the designer's work and practice, such as local or world events, personal circumstances, other designers and design movements, relationships, clients, nature, the environment and sustainability, science and technology |

## Question 7 examples

### Example A

Identify **two designs** by different designers that you have studied who have worked in the same design area.

(a) With reference to these two selected designs, comment on:

- function
- materials and/or techniques
- visual impact.

Which of the two designs is most effective? Give **two** justified reasons.

**Total marks   10**

(b) Select **one designer** from part (a).

Identify **two** influences on this designer **and** describe how these influences can be seen in any of their work.

**Total marks   5**

### Example B

Identify **two designs** by different designers that you have studied who have worked in the same design area.

(a) With reference to these two selected designs, comment on:

- visual impact
- fitness for purpose
- target market/audience.

Which of the two designs is the most appealing? Give **two** justified reasons.

**Total marks   10**

(b) Select **one designer** from part (a).

Identify **two** influences on this designer **and** describe how these influences can be seen in any of their work.

**Total marks   5**

### Example C

Identify **two designs** by different designers that you have studied who have worked in the same design area.

(a) With reference to these two selected designs, comment on:

- materials and/or techniques
- fitness for purpose
- style.

Which of the two designs is the most creative? Give **two** justified reasons.

**Total marks   10**

(b) Select **one designer** from part (a).

Identify **two** influences on this designer **and** describe how these influences can be seen in any of their work.

**Total marks   5**

### Example D

Identify **two designs** by different designers that you have studied who have worked in the same design area.

(a) With reference to these two selected designs, comment on:

- function
- style
- target market/audience.

Which of the two designs is the most successful? Give **two** justified reasons.

**Total marks   10**

(b) Select **one designer** from part (a).

Identify **two** influences on this designer **and** describe how these influences can be seen in any of their work.

**Total marks   5**

## Question 7 example answers

## Response to example A

| Darren's first attempt – a basic response | Teacher's notes |
|---|---|
| (a) Two product designs by different designers are the Cobweb Table Lamp by Louis Comfort Tiffany, designed around 1900, and the Anglepoise lamp by George Carwadine, designed in 1932. | |
| Both designs are designed to give light and illumination. One is a table lamp and the other is a desk lamp. | You need to go into more detail about their function. |
| The Tiffany lamp is made of stained glass and bronze. It is very detailed. The Anglepoise lamp is made of metal and a special spring, which Carwadine designed. | It isn't enough to give a list of materials – you need to discuss the effect of the materials and how they are used. You could also consider issues like cost and suitability. |
| The Cobweb lamp has visual impact as it is colourful and decorative. The Anglepoise lamp is more plain. | Think about how you can expand on this. Visual impact is about aesthetics – consider other aesthetic issues, such as influences and sources of inspiration. |
| I think the Anglepoise design is the most effective for a desk lamp, but the Cobweb lamp would make a better table lamp. | This is a valid point, but you need to explain the reasons to get the marks. |
| (b) Tiffany was an American designer who was born in 1848. | This part of the question asks you to write about how influences can be seen in the designer's work. |
| His father was the famous jeweller, Charles Tiffany, the owner of Tiffany and Co. | Think about important influences (e.g. Art Nouveau) and how this affected his work. |
| He started Tiffany Studios in 1890 and became famous for making his glassware. | Do not include any facts which you cannot connect to the designer's work. |

## COMMON MISTAKES

Candidates often lose marks because they do not develop points made. Try to get into the habit of making a point and then adding an explanation or justification.

## HINTS & TIPS

As the question requires you to write about two designs, it is easier to do this with designs that have a similar purpose, for example, two chairs, two lights, two posters, two bridges, two examples of outfits for women, two neckpieces, two shoe designs, two examples of packaging, etc.

| Darren's next attempt – a more in-depth and effective response | Marks |
|---|---|

(a) Two product designs by different designers are the Cobweb Table Lamp by Louis Comfort Tiffany, designed around 1900, and the Anglepoise lamp by George Carwadine, designed in 1932.

Function

Both designs give light and illumination but for different purposes. The function of the Tiffany lamp is to be used on a table to create ambient lighting in one area of a room. It also has a decorative function as it is very ornamental in style. ✓ ✓

The Anglepoise is a desk lamp which can be used for task lighting to illuminate a piece of work, for instance. ✓

Materials/Techniques

The Tiffany lamp is made of stained glass and bronze. Each lamp was handmade using traditional techniques. The method was very time-consuming, which meant that the lamps were expensive to produce and buy. The stained glass gives a decorative effect and is very attractive when lit up. The glass material meant that the lamps were fragile and had to be cleaned and handled carefully. ✓ ✓ ✓

The Anglepoise lamp is made of metal, which is tough and durable. Carwadine designed a special spring, which meant that the lamp could be repositioned without it moving back to its original place. This meant that the lamp could be used in a variety of different positions and made it very versatile and functional. The lamps could also be mass-produced which kept the costs down. ✓ ✓ ✓

Visual Impact

The Cobweb lamp has visual impact as it is colourful and decorative. The lamps were popular in the early 1900s for their typical Art Nouveau styling. This was when product designers were inspired by nature and organic forms. ✓

The Anglepoise lamp is more plain and industrial in appearance. Its appearance is secondary to its function. It is more like a Bauhaus design, where 'form follows function'. ✓

I think the Cobweb lamp makes the best table lamp as it creates soft, diffused lighting. However, the Anglepoise design is the most effective for a desk lamp as it can be adjusted. Both designs are classics which have stood the test of time. ✓ ✓

| | |
|---|---|

(b) Tiffany was influenced by the Arts & Crafts movement. These designers, like William Morris, believed that objects should be hand-crafted, not machine made. This influence can be seen in his work as every object is hand finished and unique. ✓ ✓

Art Nouveau was a major influence on his work. Art Nouveau designers were inspired by nature and this influence is obvious in his Favrile glassware, such as a series of vases with organic forms with decoration including peacock feathers and flowers. ✓ ✓

The influence of Art Nouveau can also be seen in the Cobweb lamp. Line was an important feature of Art Nouveau and the decoration on the Cobweb lamp has heavy black outlines created by the lead used in the stained glass technique. ✓

More than 10 justified points have been made for part (a) and you have answered part (b) effectively. You have answered on each aspect very well and your answer is clearly structured. I particularly like your conclusion, as it reflects the fact that both lamps have different functions. The Mies van der Rohe 'form follows function' quote is also used well here and shows a wide knowledge of the subject. | 15 |

## Response to example D

| Emily's response | Marks |
|---|---|
| (a) Two graphic designs by different designers are 'Pivolo' by Cassandre, designed in 1924, and 'Just Do It' by Neville Brody, which is from 1988. | |
| <u>Function</u> | |
| Both designs are advertisements. The Cassandre design is for an alcoholic drink called 'Pivolo', and the Brody design is for the sportswear company Nike and makes use of their slogan 'Just do it'. The Cassandre design is in a conventional portrait format, suggesting it was to be used as a poster or perhaps as an advertisement in a magazine. The landscape format of the Brody design suggests it is intended to be used on a billboard. | ✓ ✓ ✓ |
| <u>Style</u> | |
| Cassandre's poster reflects the Art Deco style with its simplified imagery.  The bird motif has been reduced to basic shapes but is still instantly recognisable as a magpie. The glass has also been simplified and stylised. | ✓ |
| The lettering is simple and geometric and the colours have been counter-changed which is very typical of the Art Deco style. | ✓ |
| Brody's design is a bold 80's style combining photographic imagery and overlapping typography. The layout is unconventional with images and text coming from different directions to create a dynamic style. | ✓ |
| <u>Target Audience</u> | |
| The Cassandre design is aimed at adults who might consume the product. The poster has a 'fun' style and would have been fashionable in its day, which suggests that the target audience was young, style-conscious adults who liked to try new things. | ✓ |
| The Brody design is also aimed at a young audience, perhaps teens to early 20s. The design is split down the middle and combines photography and typography. The text runs in different directions suggesting movement, and the close-up shot of the face gives the poster a dynamic look. The choice of words, such as 'bounce' and 'slam', also helps to convey the sporty message and appeal to the young audience. | ✓ ✓ |
| I think the Brody poster requires prior knowledge of the brand, as the actual product shots are quite small and hidden among the text. For this reason, I do not think it is the most suitable for its purpose. In my opinion, the Cassandre poster is the most suitable for its purpose, as it gives a very clear message and it is obvious what is being advertised because of the prominent lettering and imagery. | ✓ ✓ |

(b) The most important influence on Cassandre's work and practice was the Art Deco movement which became popular in Europe in the 1920s. One of the most iconic posters in the Art Deco style is Normandie, which was designed to advertise a transatlantic cruise. The ship is portrayed using simplified shapes and a limited colour palette of red, white and blue, which is typical of Art Deco style. Every detail has been simplified, including birds flying ahead of the ship. Even the lettering is a simple sans serif design typical of the Art Deco style.

✓

✓

Travel was another important influence on Cassandre's work. Advances in technology meant that travel by boat, trains and automobile was becoming accessible to wealthy people. Many of Cassandre's designs from this period are related to travel, such as his posters for the Nord Express railway line, which promote rail travel with their simplified imagery of trains and train tracks. Normandie is another example of a poster which is influenced by travel, with its striking and memorable image of a towering cruise ship.

✓

✓

✓

More than 10 justified points have been made for part (a) and you have answered part (b) very effectively. This is a well-constructed answer showing good understanding of the concepts. Good idea to answer on function first. Well done!

15

## Questions 8–12: Design studies personal choice question

You will choose to answer **one question** from this selection. Each question has a related image.

You can expect to find questions on the following design areas in the paper:

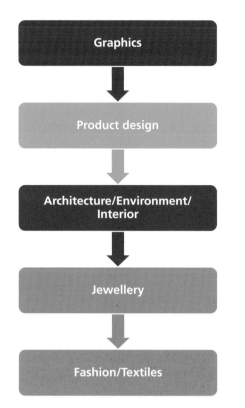

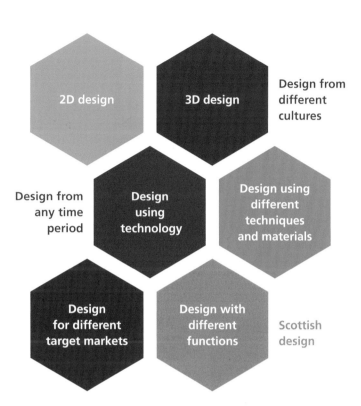

It makes sense to select the question that relates to the area you have been covering in your design portfolio. This is because each design area has its own specialist terminology. Also, if you have been involved in a particular area of design in your own practical work, you should have a deeper understanding of the issues.

## Critical analysis example questions

### Graphic design

In graphic design questions, you may be asked about designs for posters, stamps, packaging, book jackets, magazine covers, leaflets and web pages.

UN Economic and Social Development stamp designs

## Example A

Comment on these stamp designs, referring to:

■ layout
■ imagery
■ colour.

How effective are these stamp designs? Give **two** justified reasons.

**Total marks    10**

Packaging design for Doves Farm cereals (2012) designed by Studio H

## Example B

Comment on these packaging designs, referring to:

■ imagery
■ text
■ colour.

What is the target market for this packaging design? Give **two** justified reasons.

**Total marks    10**

*Women of Britain* poster (1941) designed by Donald Zec

## Example C

Comment on this poster design, referring to:

■ layout
■ text
■ imagery.

How well has the designer created a poster with visual impact? Give **two** justified reasons.

**Total marks    10**

## Response to example B

| Sanna's response | Marks |
|---|---|
| <u>Imagery</u><br><br>The imagery used in these two co-ordinating designs for cereal packaging suggests plants and growth. The Cocoa Rice box also incorporates birds and monkeys which makes me think of the rainforest. It also gives an exotic look. The designers probably wanted to give the idea of where chocolate comes from.<br><br>The Fibre Flakes box has plants you might find here, such as dandelions, as well as a butterfly. It suggests farmland. The butterfly makes you think that the product must be grown without pesticides. The imagery is stylised and simplified. It reminds me of Art Deco graphics.<br><br>Both designs also have a photograph – a product shot of the cereal from a bird's eye view. This lets the consumer see what it looks like. | ✓<br><br>✓<br><br><br>✓<br><br>✓<br><br><br>✓ |
| <u>Text</u><br><br>The text is quite understated. It includes the company logo, the name of the cereal and the fact that it is gluten free. In the layout, this is all placed prominently along the top of the box so that it is easily read. The font is a classic-looking sans-serif style which co-ordinates with the imagery nicely. | ✓<br><br>✓ |
| <u>Visual Impact</u><br><br>The colour scheme works well. Both boxes have earthy colours, which means they will look good sitting together on a supermarket shelf. The colours help give the product an identity. The brown background is an obvious choice for the chocolate-flavoured cereal. The muted colours suggest that the product is natural and does not use chemicals or additives. It makes it seem healthy. | ✓<br>✓<br>✓ |
| <u>Target Market</u><br><br>I think the target market for this cereal is young, health-conscious adults, as the design is quite sophisticated. It may also appeal to children because of the animals, but I don't think this is the main target market as you would expect it to be more colourful. I think the design also looks expensive, so it may appeal to those who don't mind paying extra for a luxury product. | ✓<br>✓ |
| A very full answer. More than 10 points have been made with all personal observations and opinions well justified. Your response demonstrates a good understanding of graphic design issues.<br><br>Your answer is well written and you have packed in a lot of points without repeating yourself. | 10 |

Mark II stacking chairs (1962) by Robin Day
Injection-moulded polypropylene shell on a metal
base (73.7 cm × 53.3 cm × 41.9 cm)

## Example D

Comment on this chair design, referring to:

- fitness for purpose
- style
- materials.

What is the target market for these chairs?
Give **two** justified reasons.

**Total marks    10**

# Product design

In this question, you could be asked about any
type of product. Possibilities include furniture,
lighting, household products and technological
products.

Radio in a bag (1981) by Daniel Weil
Transistor radio components in a printed plastic
PVC bag (29 cm × 20.7 cm × 3 cm)

## Example E

Comment on this design for a radio,
referring to:

- fitness for purpose
- materials
- target market.

What is your opinion on the style of this
radio? Give **two** justified reasons.

**Total marks    10**

## Example F

Comment on this teapot design, referring to:

- source of inspiration
- fitness for purpose
- materials.

Who might buy this teapot? Give **two** justified
reasons.

**Total marks    10**

Teapot (1892) by R. & W. Sorley, Glasgow
Silver (14 cm × 21 cm × 12.7 cm)

## Response to example D

| Darren's first attempt – a basic response | Teacher's notes |
|---|---|
| These chairs are fit for purpose. They look functional as they stack up. | You need to respond in more detail. Think of issues that affect function. |
| The style is quite ordinary. You see chairs like this every day. | |
| They are made of an injection-moulded polypropylene shell on a metal base. | This is true, but you need to expand on this point. You won't get marks for giving information from the question without expanding on it. |
| I think the target market for these chairs is everyone. | Try to justify this point with two reasons. |

| Darren's next attempt | Marks |
|---|---|
| I think these chairs are fit for purpose. They have been cleverly designed to stack up, which will save space when they are not in use. They look comfortable, as they seem to have been moulded to fit the body and it looks as if they have an optional padded cushion, which will add to the comfort. The legs have what looks like rubber stoppers on the ends. I think this is probably so that the floor doesn't get damaged. | ✓ ✓ ✓ ✓ |
| The style is quite ordinary. You see chairs like this every day but it is surprising that these were designed in 1962, so I think they must have been ahead of their time in terms of style. The form is quite organic looking as there are no sharp edges. It is good that they appear to come in a range of colours as this will allow consumers to buy the colours that suit them best. | ✓ ✓ ✓ |
| The chairs are made of an injection-moulded polypropylene shell on a metal base. The plastic material is ideal as it is lightweight, so it will be easy to move the chairs to stack them. Plastic is waterproof and can be washed to keep it clean. This material can also be formed into any shape and is low cost, which will keep the price down. The metal legs look like tubular steel which will also help to keep the design lightweight. | ✓ ✓ ✓ ✓ |
| I think the target market for these chairs is everyone. You see them in so many places, such as schools and offices, although I think they are less likely to be used in the home as they are more functional than decorative. I have even seen small versions which can be used by primary age children. | ✓ ✓ |
| Much better, Darren! Over 10 points have been made and this is a very effective answer which covers the main points well. | 10 |

## Response to example F

| Becky's first attempt – a basic response | Teacher's notes |
|---|---|
| I think this teapot looks like a thistle. It looks quite fun. | You have noticed the main source of inspiration – you just need more detail. |
| It looks fit for purpose but the handle might get hot. | Good point – but what is the reason for this? Can you think of any other points? Think about how it might have been made. |
| The teapot is made of silver, so I think it would be expensive to buy. | |
| I think people who like Scottish things might buy the teapot. | This is about target market – personal style, age group, gender, income bracket, etc. |

| Becky's next attempt | Marks |
|---|---|
| I think the source of inspiration for this teapot must have been a thistle. The form is clearly based on the shape of a thistle. There is a lot of attention to detail, with the repeating overlapping pattern found on the thistle flower worked into the surface of the teapot. This looks like diamond shapes and adds interest and decoration to the design. The handle on the lid is also a small thistle and this motif is repeated on top of the handle. The lid also seems to have been engraved with thistle leaves. Perhaps the designer wanted to make something with a Scottish theme as the thistle is our national flower. | ✓ ✓ ✓ ✓ |
| Judging by the dimensions, it is quite a small teapot, maybe just big enough for one or two cups of tea. It does look fit for purpose as the spout looks well designed and as if it would pour well. However, the handle could get hot as it is made of metal and metal conducts heat. The handle on the lid will mean that it is easier to lift, although this might get hot as well as it is made of metal. | ✓ ✓ ✓ |
| The teapot is made of silver, so I think it would be expensive to buy as this is an expensive material. The teapot looks as if it has been made by a craftsperson who has moulded and engraved the silver into this complicated design. This would add to the cost of the piece. | ✓ ✓ |
| I think the teapot would appeal to females more than males as it looks quite dainty. Maybe it would have been used by wealthy ladies for afternoon tea at the time it was made. I imagine it appealing to more mature ladies who like quirky designs. It would be a good 'conversation piece'. Perhaps it was bought as a reminder of Scotland. | ✓ ✓ |
| A much more full and detailed response and more than 10 points have been made. You have dealt with all aspects of the question very well and opinions are backed up with justification. | 10 |

# Architectural/environmental/interior design

In this question, you might be asked about buildings, bridges, shelters, interiors or other man-made structures.

Aberdeen Maritime Museum (1995) designed by Aberdeen City Council

## Example G

Comment on this architectural design, referring to:

- materials
- structure
- colour.

How well does this building fit with its surroundings? Give **two** justified reasons.

**Total marks    10**

Milwaukee Art Museum (2000) designed by Santiago Calatrava

## Example H

Comment on this design for an art gallery, referring to:

- sources of inspiration
- style
- function.

How well has the architect created a building with visual impact? Give **two** justified reasons.

**Total marks    10**

## Response to example G

| Jacob's first attempt – a basic response | Teacher's notes |
|---|---|
| This building has been constructed using glass and steel girders. There is a lot of glass. | This is a descriptive response. Try to apply what you have learned about architecture in class. |
| It is a more modern structure than the stone buildings on either side. | What else could you say about its construction? What do you remember about this type of architecture? You could also say how the structure affects the style and function. |
| A grey blue has been used, maybe to help it blend in with its surroundings. | Try to give more detail here. |
| This building is different from its surroundings but doesn't look out of place. | You need to give two reasons why this is the case. |

| Jacob's next attempt | Marks |
|---|---|
| This building has been constructed using glass and steel girders. This gives a modern, industrial look which is in contrast to the buildings made with more traditional stone on either side. There is a lot of glass used. This means the building is light inside and will make the most of the view. | ✓ ✓ |
| The Maritime Museum is a more modern structure than the stone buildings on either side. It has been constructed using the curtain wall technique. This was a method first used by Bauhaus designers and involved the use of steel girders and pillars to create a load-bearing structure. This meant that the wall no longer had to hold the building up, so for the first time large glass windows could be used all around the building. In the interior of the building, the steel girders have been left exposed, maybe as a reminder of the shipbuilding of the past. The girders have round holes cut in them. This would reduce the weight, but also reminds me of port holes, a maritime symbol. Curves are used to soften the straight lines of the girders in the interior and exterior. | ✓ ✓ ✓ ✓ |
| The entrance is a revolving door. These are good at allowing the traffic to flow but keep the cold out, which would be important in a cold and windy location . | ✓ |
| In the interior, a neutral grey blue has been used, which reflects the colours in the environment. This means that the building blends in well with its surroundings without being too obvious. | ✓ |
| This building is very different in style from its surroundings but doesn't look out of place. The large panels of glass reflecting the surroundings also help in this respect. The entrance is small and unobtrusive and there is no obvious signage, which helps the building disappear into its environment. | ✓ ✓ |
| A very good response which shows your understanding of architecture. | 10 |

# Jewellery design

In jewellery design questions, you may be asked about designs for neckpieces, brooches, bracelets and cuffs, crowns and tiaras, belt buckles, watches and any other body adornments.

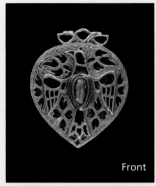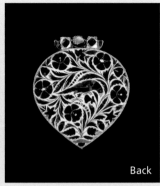

Front

Back

Pendant from India (17ᵗʰ century) by an unknown designer
Gold, diamond, rubies, emeralds, enamel
(Height: 3.7 cm)

## Example I

Comment on this pendant design, referring to:

- sources of inspiration
- style
- materials.

Who might have worn this piece of jewellery? Give **two** justified reasons.

**Total marks   10**

Brooch (1901) designed by Georges Fouquet
Gold and enamel
(13 cm × 6.1 cm)

## Example J

Comment on this brooch design, referring to:

- sources of inspiration
- materials
- target market.

What is your opinion on the style of this piece? Give **two** justified reasons.

**Total marks   10**

Inflection V/1 neckpiece (1988) designed by David Watkins
Gilded brass, blue and red Colorcore
(Diameter: 31.4 cm)

## Example K

Comment on this design for a neckpiece, referring to:

- sources of inspiration
- style
- practicality.

What target market might this piece be aimed at? Give **two** justified reasons.

**Total marks   10**

| Robyn's response | Marks |
|---|---|
| <u>Sources of Inspiration</u><br><br>I would guess that the source of inspiration for this neckpiece was something man-made and mechanical. The shapes and forms remind me of clockwork machinery or cogs and wheels. | ✓ |
| <u>Style</u><br><br>The style is modern. It is a bold piece of jewellery because of the large scale. It definitely has visual impact. The main element used is shape. The shapes are regular and geometric. The repeating shapes create a bold pattern. The piece appears to be constructed of two flat pieces, one made of brass and the other of a coloured material. The flat blue of the section underneath contrasts with the warm tones of the brass section on top. These are unconventional materials for jewellery and give an unusual appearance to the neckpiece. | ✓<br>✓<br>✓<br><br>✓ |
| <u>Practicality</u><br><br>The neckpiece is not ergonomic; it has not been designed to fit the body. In many ways, it looks quite uncomfortable. The circular form just sits around the neck and might be quite heavy. The protruding parts may be a bit of a health and safety hazard. It is not the most practical piece of jewellery, but I don't think this was the designer's main consideration. I think it is a piece which puts style before practicality, like many fashion and jewellery pieces. | ✓<br>✓<br>✓ |
| <u>Target Market</u><br><br>I think the target market for this neckpiece would be a female collector of unusual designer jewellery. The piece certainly makes a statement and could work well with a plain black dress. I imagine it would only be worn for special occasions because of the lack of practicality. It would have to be worn by a very confident individual as the large scale would get the wearer noticed. | ✓<br><br>✓ |
| This was quite a challenging piece to discuss but you have done well. Your exam technique is very good as you have brought in related issues, such as discussing the materials in relation to the style. | 10 |

## COMMON MISTAKES

Many candidates run out of things to say when they answer the question in a very restricted way. You often need to expand your response to include related issues. As long as you always make a connection with the main issue being asked about, this is fine and you will gain marks.

## HINTS & TIPS

Remember that when you are asked about style, you can discuss how colour, shape, form, pattern and texture have been used to create the style.

# Fashion/textile design

In this question, you may be asked about designs for any fashion or textile item. Possibilities include historical fashion, catwalk creations, clothing for men, women and children, street style, costumes for theatre and film, uniforms, protective clothing. You could also be asked about textile designs for clothing and interiors.

Costume from the OVO show,
Cirque du Soleil (2009) by Liz Vandal
Printed fabric

## Example L

Comment on this costume design, referring to:

- function
- form
- materials.

How effective is the visual impact of this design? Give **two** justified reasons.

**Total marks 10**

Ensemble (1879–81) by Halling,
Pearce and Stone
Satin, trimmed with figured silk,
chenille tassels and machine-made
lace, lined with silk and cotton

## Example M

Comment on this dress design, referring to:

- form
- wearability
- materials.

Who might have worn this dress? Give **two** justified reasons.

**Total marks 10**

Firefighter's uniform (2012)
Fire-resistant materials
including aramid (Nomex),
PTEF-coated kevlar, kevlar
felt and reflective tape

## Example N

Comment on this uniform design, referring to:

- function
- materials
- style.

How effective is this design? Give **two** justified reasons.

**Total marks 10**

## Response to example N

| Amy's first descriptive response | Amy's second more analytical response |
|---|---|
| <u>Function</u> | <u>Function</u> |
| The function is a uniform for a firefighter. It has gloves, a helmet and a mask. | The function is a uniform for a firefighter. It has a protective function, so will need to be tough and durable and be able to withstand extreme conditions. There are protective gloves, boots and headwear. The helmet will protect the firefighter from falling objects. A mask is also included in case the firefighter needs to breathe in smoky conditions. It will also protect their face and eyes from debris.<br><br>As it is a uniform it also has an identity function. It is important that firefighters can recognise each other and that members of the public can tell who the firefighters are. |
| <u>Materials</u> | <u>Materials</u> |
| The materials used are fire resistant. The uniform is a dull yellow with brighter yellow stripes. | The materials used are fire resistant. This is important given the job that firefighters do. They may need to enter burning buildings and so their clothing must not be flammable. The uniform is a dull yellow with brighter yellow stripes made of reflective tape. This is so that firefighters can be seen in low visibility conditions.<br><br>The gloves and knees of the uniform look as if they are padded. This will be to protect their hands from heat and their knees if they have to crawl through small spaces or get down onto the ground. |
| <u>Style</u> | <u>Style</u> |
| The style is baggy with lots of pockets. | Practicality is more important than style, but the distinctive yellow colour, high visibility stripes and helmet make it instantly recognisable as a firefighter's uniform. The shape is baggy, presumably to make it easy to move in. There are lots of pockets to allow firefighters to carry all their equipment. |
| <u>Effectiveness</u> | <u>Effectiveness</u> |
| I think this design will be effective.<br><br>These are valid observations and opinions. Now try to develop these by thinking about reasons why. | I think this design will be effective, as uniforms like this have been used for some time now and have not been replaced with anything better. The main purpose is to protect the firefighter and it seems well designed to do this as the person's body is completely covered.<br><br>Much fuller and more detailed responses. Good work! |

# Chapter 5

# 5 Expressive Art and Design Studies Wordbanks

To complete your expressive art and design studies successfully and do well in the question paper, it is important to extend your range of vocabulary and build up a good understanding of art and design terminology.

We will start with the **visual elements**, which artists and designers use in different combinations for visual effect.

## The visual elements

### Line

Line can be used to show shape and form when drawing or painting.

Texture and pattern can be represented through line.

Line can express mood and emotion in expressive art.

In design, line can be used to communicate ideas and can affect the style of a design.

| Words about line | | | | | |
|---|---|---|---|---|---|
| thick | angular | outline | flowing | zigzag | continuous |
| thin | rectilinear | horizontal | graceful | jagged | broken |
| broad | rough | vertical | elegant | twisting | ragged |
| straight | textural | diagonal | precise | cross-hatched | scratchy |
| curved | expressive | wavy | accurate | stripe | inconsistent |
| long | bold | curvilinear | sensitive | neat | freehand |
| short | confident | fluid | delicate | sketchy | gestural |
| hard | hesitant | smooth | controlled | faint | spontaneous |
| light | fine | squiggly | definite | subtle | |

### Tone

Tone can be used to show the variation from light to dark.

Tone can be used in drawing to describe 3D form, pattern and texture.

The direction and source of light in a drawing or painting can be shown through tone.

Tone can be used expressively or to create a sense of realism or to show mood and atmosphere.

**Words about tone**

| | | | | | |
|---|---|---|---|---|---|
| light | highlight | limited tonal range | dramatic | hard light | drab |
| dark | half-tone | wide tonal range | contrasting | diffused light | faded |
| soft | mid-tone | tonal value | exaggerated | high key | sombre |
| subtle | monotone | tonal scale | hard | low key | gloomy |
| muted | graduated | light source | glowing | reflected light | murky |
| gradation | graded | direction of light | luminous | reflection | dim |
| blended | shaded | shadow | illuminated | bright | flat |

## Colour

Colour can convey mood in expressive art.

We often associate colour with emotion.

Colour can be used to enhance a design or to attract a certain target market.

In design, colour can contribute to style.

**Words about colour**

| | | | |
|---|---|---|---|
| primary | transparent | bright | monochromatic |
| secondary | opaque | strong | neutral |
| tertiary | hue | harsh | subtle |
| complementary | pigment | vibrant | restrained |
| opposite | tone | intense | limited palette |
| contrasting | tint | saturated | restricted palette |
| harmonious | balanced | bold | pale |
| related | varied | deep | muted |
| hot/warm | deep | vivid | faded |
| cold/cool | fluorescent | rich | realistic |
| symbolic | luminescent | expressive | naturalistic |
| decorative | pearlescent | exaggerated | life-like |
| advancing | iridescent | clashing | earthy |
| receding | lurid | gaudy | delicate |
| balanced | loud | garish | weak |
| blended | brilliant | polychromatic | washed out |
| reflected colour | kaleidoscopic | multi-coloured | pure |

## The colour wheel

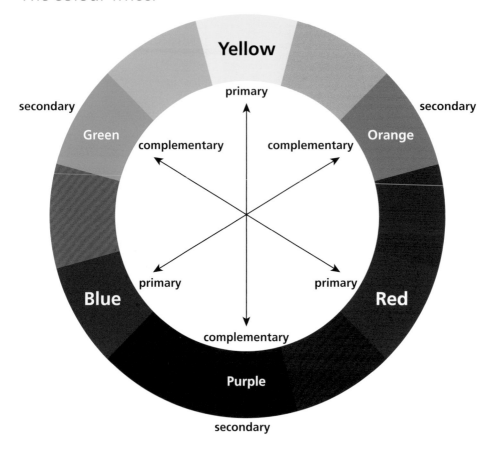

### Primary colours

Primary colours cannot be mixed using other colours. Red, yellow and blue are primary colours.

### Harmonious colours

These are the groups of colours that are next to each other on the colour wheel – for example, green, turquoise and blue, or red, orange and yellow. They are sometimes called analogous colours.

### Complementary colours

Complementary colours are opposite each other on the colour wheel. For this reason, they are sometimes called opposite colours. When used together, they tend to clash.

## Secondary colours

Secondary colours are made by mixing two primary colours. These are purple (blue and red), orange (red and yellow) and green (blue and yellow).

## Tertiary colours

Tertiary colours are made by mixing the three primary colours together. Depending on the amount of each colour, different results will be achieved. Tertiary colours are a variety of browns or greys.

## Tints, tones and shades

Tints are made by adding a colour to white.

Tones are made by adding grey to a colour.

Shades are made by adding black to a colour.

## Texture

Texture can be used to describe how a surface feels or looks.

Texture can be represented using 2D techniques.

3D techniques can be used to create surface texture.

| Words about texture | | | |
|---|---|---|---|
| tactile | furry | even | brushstroke |
| touch | scaly | uneven | impasto |
| textural | silky | grainy | bas relief |
| soft | hairy | indented | low relief |
| hard | rippled | pitted | linear |
| rough | wrinkled | dusty | swirling |
| smooth | crinkled | waxy | dashed |
| coarse | ribbed | greasy | directional |
| fine | grooved | velvety | random |
| flat | spiky | fleecy | bumpy |
| shiny | scratched | woolly | woven |
| glossy | abrasive | matt | |

# Shape

Shape defines a two-dimensional area.

Shape can help to communicate design ideas and can contribute to the style of a design.

Shapes can be repeated to make patterns.

# Form

Form is three-dimensional shape.

Form can be used in sculpture, low relief work or in 3D design.

In expressive art, form can be used to show realism.

In design, form can contribute to style.

| sphere | cube | cylinder | cone | pyramid |

| Words about shape and form | | | | |
|---|---|---|---|---|
| **Shape and form** | | **Shape** | **Form** | |
| regular | simple | circular | sphere | sculptural |
| irregular | complex | rectangular | cube | architectural |
| geometric | fragmented | oblong | cylinder | profile |
| organic | jagged | square | pyramid | relief |
| man-made | pointed | triangular | cone | moulded |
| natural | distorted | oval | conical | sculpted |
| angular | freeform | pentagon | helix | modelled |
| rounded | bold | hexagon | spherical | carved |
| symmetrical | distinct | octagon | cuboid | built |
| asymmetrical | indistinct | outlined | triangular | constructed |
| flat | spiral | positive | tactile | assembled |
| repeating | twisted | negative | textural | tool marks |
| elongated | large-scale | overlapping | massive | solid |
| simplified | small-scale | silhouette | monumental | hard |
| stylised | short | negative space | hollow | |
| spiky | tall | amorphous | light | |
| hard-edged | wide | nebulous | heavy | |
| soft | narrow | fluid | mass | |

## Pattern

Pattern is an arrangement of repeating elements or motifs: lines; shapes; forms; tones; or colours.

Pattern can be used to enhance expressive artwork or design ideas.

Pattern can be found in the natural and man-made environments.

| Words about pattern | | | |
|---|---|---|---|
| applied | random | dots | decorative |
| repeating | varied | polka dot | ornate |
| simple | regular | dashes | ornamental |
| complex | linear | lines | embellished |
| man-made | rectilinear | stripes | bold |
| natural | curvilinear | chequered | subtle |
| geometric | rhythmic | tartan | clashing |
| organic | symmetrical | plaid | kinetic |
| mechanical | asymmetrical | floral | optical |
| motifs | symbols | speckled | digital |
| squiggles | mirror image | marbled | abstract |
| large-scale | multi-directional | cross-hatched | psychedelic |
| small-scale | half-drop | stippled | tessellated |

# Expressive art

## Composition

Composition is the arrangement of elements within a painting, drawing or photograph.

In sculpture, composition is about the spatial arrangement of 3D forms.

Artists use composition to lead the viewer's eye around the work in a particular way.

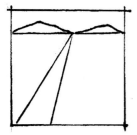 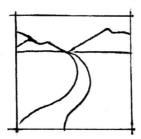 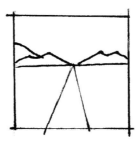 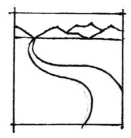

| Words about composition | | | | |
|---|---|---|---|---|
| arrangement | viewpoint | focal point | subject | sitter (in portraiture) |
| foreground | framed | centre of interest | object | subject matter |
| middleground | cropped | point(s) of interest | distorted | frame within frame |
| background | close-up | elevated viewpoint | fragmented | in proportion |
| horizontal | wide angle | camera angle | symmetrical | out of proportion |
| vertical | circular | eye-level | asymmetrical | portrait orientation |
| diagonal | triangular | bird's eye view | balanced | landscape orientation |
| linear | staged | low viewpoint | busy | one-point perspective |
| horizon line | set up | picture plane | cluttered | two-point perspective |
| perspective | dynamic | negative space | crowded | flattened perspective |
| leading line | small-scale | rule of thirds | minimalist | aerial perspective |
| s-curve | large-scale | depth of field | sparse | vanishing point |

## Mood and atmosphere

By using different combinations of the visual elements and a variety of techniques, artists can create a variety of different moods in their work.

| Words about mood and atmosphere | | | | |
|---|---|---|---|---|
| tranquil | exciting | atmospheric | violent | sad |
| peaceful | busy | overcast | disordered | pessimistic |
| quiet | fun | gloomy | aggressive | melancholy |
| serene | happy | sunlit | hostile | depressing |
| calm | joyful | sun-drenched | moody | dismal |
| informal | passionate | shadowy | intense | desolate |
| relaxed | flamboyant | warm | threatening | lonely |
| still | lively | cold | disturbing | sensitive |
| undisturbed | optimistic | leaden | powerful | thought provoking |
| controlled | emotional | dreary | inspiring | moving |
| dispassionate | expressive | lack-lustre | poignant | breathtaking |

# Design

## Aesthetics and style

Aesthetics is about appearance.

Each designer has their own distinctive style which affects the appearance of their designs.

Different aesthetics appeal to different target audiences.

The visual elements will affect the style of a design, so you should refer to these wordbanks as well.

| Words about aesthetics and style | | | |
|---|---|---|---|
| line | antique | gothic | appealing |
| colour | traditional | rococo | attractive |
| shape | classical | baroque | visual impact |
| form | Victoriana | romantic | decorative |
| pattern | minimalist | Arts and Crafts | ornamental |
| texture | vintage | Art Nouveau | sophisticated |
| source of inspiration | retro | Art Deco | elegant |
| influences | futuristic | modernist | sculptural |
| the 'look' | industrial | punk | tasteful |
| appearance | original | contemporary | flashy |
| layout | quirky | up-to-date | experimental |
| arrangement | idiosyncratic | sleek | eclectic |
| text | kitsch | streamlined | eccentric |
| font | avant-garde | fun | statement piece |
| use of space | ahead of its time | funky | conversation piece |

# Function

Function is about the purpose of a design.

Designers have to consider functional issues, even in very decorative pieces.

| Words about function | | | |
|---|---|---|---|
| purpose | ergonomics | durability | eco-friendly |
| intention | user-friendly | fragile | sustainability |
| rationale | technological | delicate | safety |
| protoype | mechanical | built in obsolescence | risk |
| concept | high-tech | disposable | danger |
| fitness for purpose | digital | hard-wearing | hazard |
| functionality | computerised | robust | secure |
| wearability (fashion) | microtechnology | sturdy | protection |
| suitability | nanotechnology | built to last | weight |
| practicality | robotic | multi-functional | scale |

# Target market

Designers have to consider their target market, whether this is one client,
a specific group or the mass market.

| Words about target market | | | |
|---|---|---|---|
| design brief | gender | age group | cost |
| client | male | age bracket | budget |
| specification | female | babies | added value |
| commission | unisex | children | income bracket |
| one-off | designer label | teenagers | disposable income |
| limited edition | diffusion line | young adults | customer type |
| mass produced | high street | adults | socioeconomic group |
| mass-market | middle-market | couples | cost effective |
| disposable | commercial | families | status symbol |
| sustainable | trendy | general public | value for money |
| eco-friendly | fashionable | demographic | promotion |
| market research | exclusive | niche market | persuasion |
| market forces | target audience | up-market | consumer appeal |

# Chapter 6

# External Assessment: Portfolio Gallery

## Candidate A

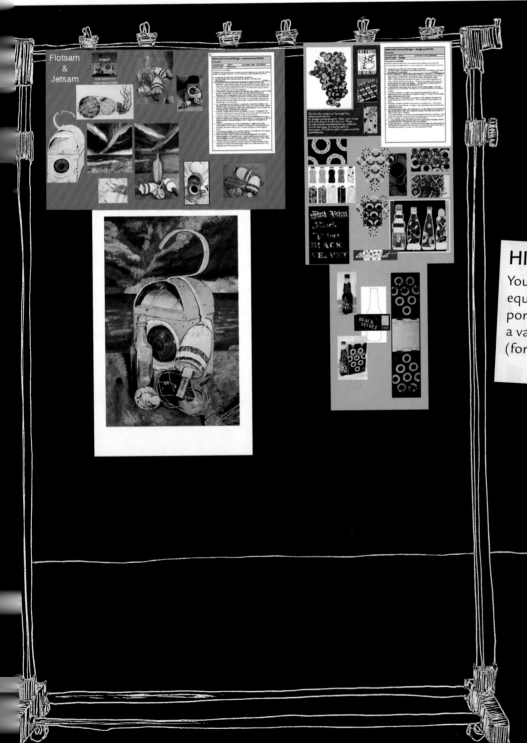

Your National 5 expressive and design portfolios are submitted to SQA to be marked. Your work is suspended from racks while it is being marked. The work from your school is hung up in alphabetical order.

### HINTS & TIPS

You are allowed to submit **up to** the equivalent of 3 × A2 sheets for each portfolio. This can be presented in a variety of formats, as appropriate (for example, 4 × A3 plus 1 × A2).

# Candidate B

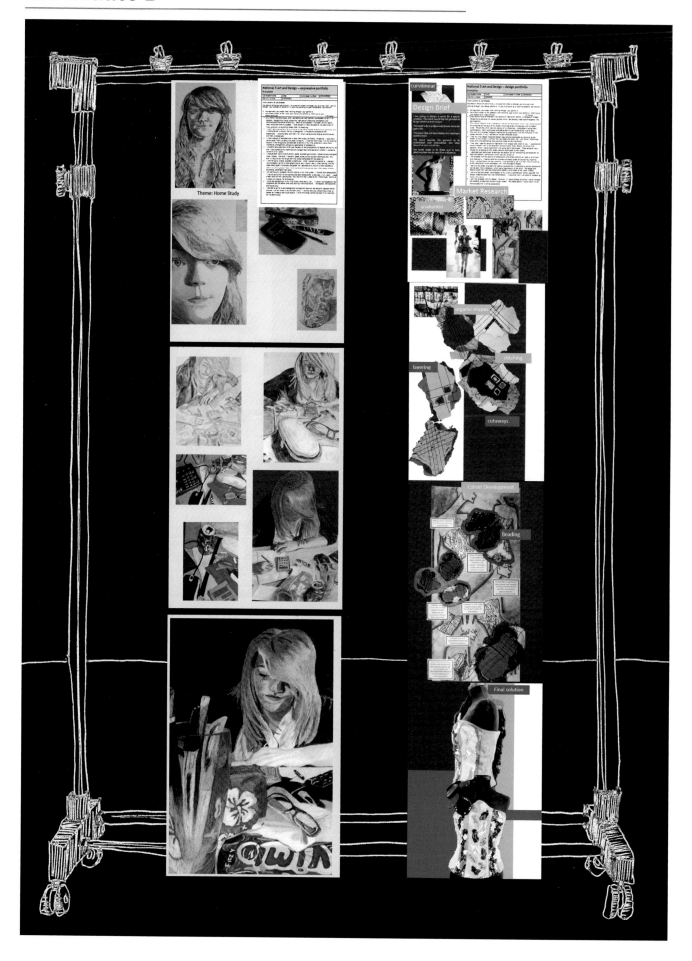

Theme: Home Study

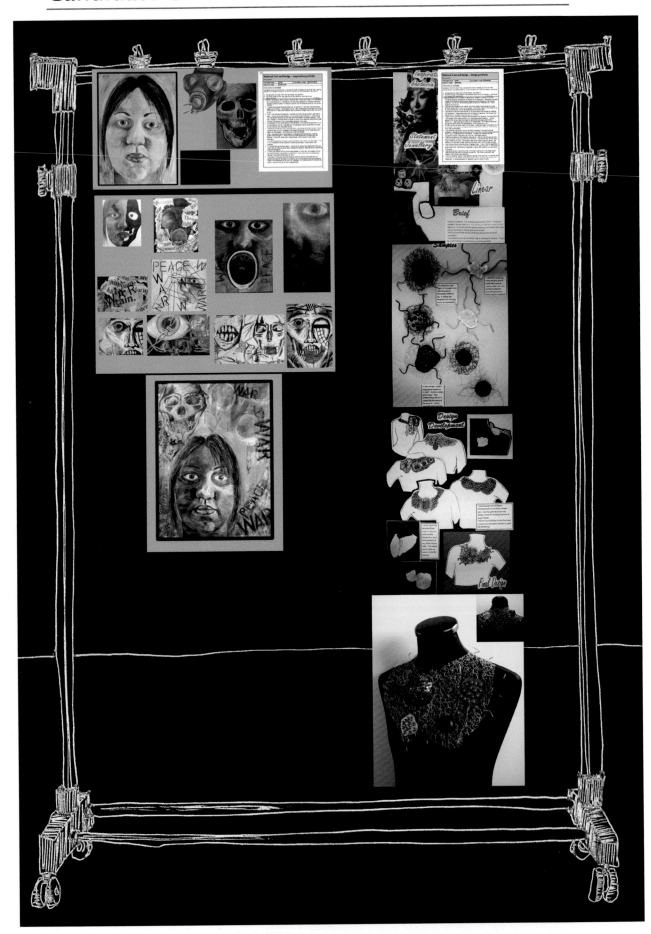

# Some possible portfolio formats

## Portfolio gallery

## Possible portfolio formats

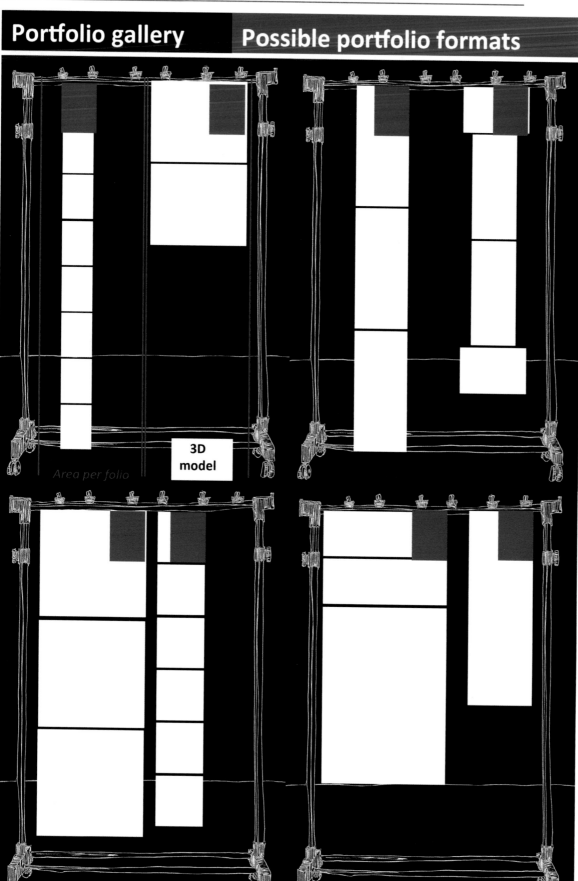

Area per folio

3D model

Key - SQA evaluation form

# Chapter 7

# Useful Resources

| | |
|---|---|
| National Gallery | www.nationalgallery.org.uk |
| National Portrait Gallery | www.npg.org.uk |
| Tate Galleries | www.tate.org.uk |
| British Museum | www.britishmuseum.org |
| Crafts Council | www.craftscouncil.org.uk |
| Design Museum | www.designmuseum.org |
| Victoria & Albert Museum | www.vam.ac.uk |
| Design Council | www.designcouncil.org.uk |
| National Gallery, Scotland | www.nationalgalleries.org |
| Pompidou Centre, Paris | www.centrepompidou.fr |
| Guggenheim Museum | www.guggenheim.org |
| Museum of Modern Art, New York | www.moma.org |
| Courtauld Gallery | www.courtauld.ac.uk/gallery |
| Institute of Contemporary Art | www.ica.org.uk |
| Saatchi Gallery | www.saatchigallery.com |
| White Cube | www.whitecube.com |
| Flowers Gallery | www.flowersgallery.com |
| Imperial War Museums | www.iwm.org.uk |
| British Journal of Photography | www.bjp-online.com |
| National Science and Media Museum | www.nationalmediamuseum.org.uk |
| Magnum Photos | www.magnumphotos.com |
| Art Cyclopedia | www.artcyclopedia.com |
| WebMuseum (online art gallery) | www.ibiblio.org/wm |
| Museum and gallery websites collection | www.gallerywebsites.co.uk |
| Pinterest (image website) | www.pinterest.com |
| The Costume Gallery (historical fashion and costume) | www.costumegallery.com |
| International Feltmakers Association | www.feltmakers.com |
| The 62 Group of Textile Artists | www.62group.org.uk |
| Public Monuments and Sculpture Association | www.pmsa.org.uk |
| Dazzle Exhibitions (jewellery) | www.dazzle-exhibitions.com |
| Velvet da Vinci (contemporary jewellery) | www.velvetdavinci.com |
| Klimt 02 (contemporary jewellery) | www.klimt02.net |
| Graphics (packaging design) | www.lovelypackage.com/ |
| Farfetch (fashion) | www.farfetch.com/uk/ |
| British Vogue magazine | www.vogue.co.uk |
| Royal Institute of British Architects | www.architecture.com |
| Architectural Association | www.aaschool.ac.uk |

# Acknowledgements

We would like to thank a number of people who made this book possible:

The art and design pupils of James Hamilton Academy, Mearns Castle High School and Kilmarnock Academy, with particular thanks to Sanna Ahmad, Robyn Anderson, Eamon Grady, Amy Murray, Emily Raine, Beth Wilson and Darren Wylie for the examples of artwork, Nicolle Phillips for the cover photograph, and to Anna Cunningham, Aimee McCabe and David Cameron for contributing photographs.

Our head teachers, Janis Teale and Dean Smith, who continue to value and support art and design education.

John Mitchell and Elizabeth Fletcher at Hodder Gibson for having faith in our original vision.

Our colleagues at school and SQA for being passionate about art and design and for contributing to the development of the approaches in this book, with special mention to Asmara Azeem, Tia Campbell, Gaynor Catterson, Zandra Gatti, Andy Latto, Hugh Mackay, Kirsty McKee, Susan Miller, David Marshall and Caroline Stewart.

Last, but certainly not least, thanks to John Kirkland, Andy and Josh Lightbown (and Diesel the dog!) for putting up with being neglected during the writing of this book.

  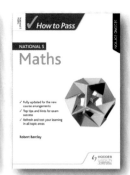